PRAISE FOR *DAT*

'Shorful Islam has a unique ability to make the complex simple. In true form, *Data Culture* is a highly accessible guide with practical tips and compelling examples to help make building a data culture an achievable goal. It is a must-read for data leaders who aspire to increase their influence and maximize the impact of their role. It is also highly relevant for C-suite leaders who want to cut through the noise and harness data to improve business performance.'
Chris Daplyn, Global Chief Executive, MMT Digital

'Shorful Islam shares his unique perspective on data leadership combined with insights on the organizational and human psychology of change. His experiences are invaluable for any leader driving organizational transformation.'
Sanjeevan Bala, Global Chief Data and AI Officer, ITV

'Most organizations aspire to be data-driven, but this doesn't happen just because you have data being collected somewhere in the building. The expectations and behaviours about how an organization uses its data to become wiser and more successful depend on the data culture that it fosters, across the business and especially in its leadership. Shorful Islam's *Data Culture* explores the critical contribution that data culture makes to success and how to create and foster a healthy data culture that makes data central to decision making. As data availability expands exponentially, the culture around its use becomes ever-more important to understand and Shorful's experience across academia, public and private sector work makes him an expert guide.'
Stephen Woodford, CEO, Advertising Association

'An essential exploration of the transformative power of data within organizations. This book is a blueprint for building a data-centric organization. Shorful Islam articulates why merely having analysts and the latest technology falls short if the organizational culture does not embrace data at its core.'
Annelies Jansen, Founder, Equals Three

'Shorful Islam encapsulates his exceptional experience, skills and wisdom in this book. Anyone who operates with or near data knows how much data culture matters to effectiveness, and how little has been written about it. The observations in *Data Culture* are gems.'
Dominic Cameron, Executive Chairman, CovertSwarm

'The more connected the world becomes, the more it generates a blizzard of data every second. Many organizations are operating in a state of informed bewilderment. They know everything but understand little. Shorful Islam has used his many years of hard-won wisdom as a data leader, and deep knowledge of psychology, to create this much-needed guide to successfully navigate developing a strong data culture. *Data Culture* will help data leaders develop the right culture for their organization.'
Darren Savage, Honorary Teaching Fellow and Marketer in Residence, Lancaster University

'Shorful Islam is a rare leader. He mentors naturally without even thinking about it. *Data Culture* is a must for anyone needing to get their business on board with making being "data-driven" who they are.'
Carolyn Bondi, Founder, The Thread Team, and Co-Chair, DMA Customer Data Council

Data Culture

Develop an effective
data-driven organization

Shorful Islam

KoganPage

First published in Great Britain and the United States in 2024 by Kogan Page Limited

2nd Floor, 45 Gee Street
London
EC1V 3RS
United Kingdom

8 W 38th Street, Suite 902
New York, NY 10018
USA

www.koganpage.com

Kogan Page books are printed on paper from sustainable forests.

ISBNs

Hardback   978 1 3986 1422 2
Paperback   978 1 3986 1420 8
Ebook   978 1 3986 1421 5

British Library Cataloguing-in-Publication Data
A CIP record for this book is available from the British Library.

Library of Congress Cataloging-in-Publication Data
Names: Islam, Shorful, author.
Title: Data culture : develop an effective data-driven organization / Shorful Islam.
Description: London ; New York, NY : KoganPage , 2024. | Includes bibliographical references and index.
Identifiers: LCCN 2024006386 (print) | LCCN 2024006387 (ebook) | ISBN 9781398614222 (hardback) | ISBN 9781398614208 (paperback) | ISBN 9781398614215 (ebook)
Subjects: LCSH: Knowledge management. | Decision making–Data processing. | Information technology–Management. | Corporate culture. | Organizational change.
Classification: LCC HD30.2 .I843 2024 (print) | LCC HD30.2 (ebook) | DDC 658.4/038–dc23/eng/20240312
LC record available at https://lccn.loc.gov/2024006386
LC ebook record available at https://lccn.loc.gov/2024006387

Typeset by Integra Software Services, Pondicherry
Print production managed by Jellyfish
Printed and bound by CPI Group (UK) Ltd, Croydon CR0 4YY

'Actions are but by intention.'
To my mum and dad, who gave me faith.

CONTENTS

LIST OF FIGURES
AND TABLES

Figures

Tables

ABOUT THE AUTHOR

Shorful Islam is the co-founder and CEO of Be Data Solutions and the founder of Subatomic Analytics. He also serves as the Data and Behavioural Science Advisor to OutThink, and Data and AI Advisor to Beam, Fit For Work and Data Ravens. With over 20 years of industry experience in data analytics and data science, Islam has helped some of the world's largest companies with their data strategies. He has headed up data analytics teams at a range of institutions and organizations spanning the NHS, local government, ITV, adam&eveDDB and Wunderman. With his strength in starting, growing and nurturing teams, Islam is experienced in building data cultures within organizations, allowing data analysts and data scientists to thrive. He has a PhD in psychology.

CONTRIBUTORS

Stephen Kinsella, Director, Analytics and Technologies at dmg media

Julie Screech, an independent data strategy and tech consultant

Fayez Shriwardhankar, Head of Data at Raconteur

Lara Izlan, Director of Insights and Analytics at ITV

Min Bhogaita, ex Director of Analytics at Deloitte

Abs Owdud, Analytics Director at Digitas UK

Adam Wright, Chief Data Officer at Oodle Car Finance

FOREWORD

We are often told that we live in the age of information, and that data is the 'new oil', the currency that fuels progress and understanding. However, whilst most organizations appreciate its worth, few get to experience its true value without first fostering an environment where data is considered a creative asset as well as a strategic one.

In the rapidly evolving landscape of information and technology businesses, cultivating a robust data culture is paramount, but few achieve it. This book serves as a guide through the intricate challenges of developing a data culture, offering insights, strategies and, most importantly, real-world examples from hard-won experiences to inspire individuals from the data analyst to the C-suite and whole organizations to develop a genuinely data-centric future.

Shorful, a humble yet brilliant man, was the person who first set me on my career path in analytics. We first met in the hallowed halls of what was then known as ITV Broadband on Grays Inn Road, London, when I was an aspiring data analyst. Shorful's pedigree both as an academic and as a business leader in the field of data has always spoken for itself; however, I was always struck by how he always seemed to have better ideas than anyone else, but not everyone was able to see them. It is only after years of subsequent experience in the field myself that I realized why – Shorful has always been light years ahead of his time. Only upon reflecting on my time at ITV a decade later did it become apparent to me that he was articulating concepts that years later matured and were given catchy names such as Big Data and cloud computing – and then everyone understood. To this day, I am eternally grateful to him for setting me off on what has been a challenging, sometimes taxing but ultimately rewarding and enjoyable career – although he has occasionally apologized for this!

This book offers a compelling journey into the transformative power of cultivating a data-centric mindset from someone who has actually lived it and flourished. Going beyond the technicalities, readers stand to gain a profound understanding of how fostering a robust data culture can drive innovation, enhance decision-making and ultimately propel individuals and organizations toward success. Whether you are a novice or an experienced professional, this book will provide you with valuable insights that transcend industries, making it an indispensable guide for those seeking to create the conditions needed to truly thrive using data.

As we navigate this ever-changing landscape, may we benefit from Shorful's experiences and inspire a genuine cultural shift that not only harnesses the power of data but also fosters creativity, innovation, informed decision-making and a deeper understanding of the world around us.

Welcome to the journey of shaping a transformative data culture. Travel well.

Stephen Kinsella

Director of Analytics and
Data Technologies, dmg media

PREFACE

I have always wanted to write a book about data. However, I never could settle on what to write about. If I look back, even during my academic years I was always interested in data and what it meant. However, in an area that is so vast and forever evolving how do you settle on a topic? Luckily for me, when Kogan Page reached out to me to write a book, they suggested that I focus on my leadership and team-building experience, which led to settling on the topic of data culture.

For me, this captures where I believe data has the most value. It's something that, if done well, can have a profound impact on an organization and its ability to stay relevant and competitive. I have worked in many roles at different companies as well as for many companies as a consultant. This has given me significant insight into how different organizations develop, foster and maintain a data culture.

However, I didn't want this book to be a singular reflection of just my thoughts – I wanted to seek out and speak to other data leaders I had worked with over the years. I have been fortunate that many kindly gave up their time to discuss the topic of data culture and allowed their thoughts, comments and opinions to be included in the book. These insights have helped me write what I hope will be a truly insightful perspective on how to create, develop, nurture and maintain a healthy data culture in an organization.

Having lots of material to include in this book was not the hard part when writing. It has and probably always will be, for me, starting something. The last time I wrote this many words for a single publication was over 20 years ago for my PhD thesis. Since then I have written many short articles but nothing substantial. It's an interesting exercise in self discipline, making time, finding the energy and maintaining the motivation to continue writing.

As I began writing, I found that more ideas and concepts came to me, as well as a flood of real-world examples I wanted to include. I have tried to include as much practical advice in this book for data leaders as was permitted by time and word count, and I am sure there is still another book or two left in me on just this topic. I also found that my knowledge of psychology helped shape how I built data cultures in organizations, and I wanted this book to also reflect that knowledge.

There is nothing like the feeling of finishing – it's a moment of relief but also hesitation. Relief in finally finishing, but hesitation as to whether it is good enough. I hope I have done the topic justice and that the readers of this book find it valuable. For me this has been a worthwhile experience and, though tough, is one that I hope I will repeat sometime in the future.

ACKNOWLEDGEMENTS

I would like to firstly thank the many data leaders who gave up their time to share their thoughts, opinions and expertise. Their invaluable contributions have significantly enriched the content and depth of this book. I would like to extend my deepest appreciation to Stephen Kinsella, Director, Analytics and Technologies at dmg media, Julie Screech, an independent data strategy and tech consultant, Fayez Shriwardhankar, Head of Data at Raconteur, Lara Izlan, Director of Insights and Analytics at ITV, Min Bhogaita, ex Director of Analytics at Deloitte, Abs Owdud, Analytics Director at Digitas UK and Adam Wright, Chief Data Officer at Oodle Car Finance.

To my friends Nikita and Mo, and business partner Keith, thank you for your support. I would also like to express my deepest gratitude to Stephen, for his support and encouragement in writing this book, and for organizing and accompanying me on a trip around Spain that provided the necessary environment to complete the final few chapters.

To my children Tayyibah, Tauhid and Tahmid, you have enriched my life with your diverse perspectives and unending questions. Your resilience, creativity and differences are constant sources of inspiration. I am forever learning from you.

I would also like to take this opportunity to thank Kogan Page for their support in helping me write this book. I would like especially to thank Isabelle Cheng who helped me navigate to a topic for this book and to Charlie Lynn who helped me edit the book.

Finally, I am grateful to my family for their support, and for giving me the space and time to write this book, and especially my two brothers, Shomsul and Shirajul, without whom I probably would not have achieved many of the things I have done to date.

What is data culture? 1

How people interpret, manifest and practise the beliefs, values and behaviours of a culture depends on how they learnt and were exposed to that culture. Data culture is no different. Organizations have different values around data, and whereas some are healthy and represent a strong data culture, others are somewhat weak and demonstrate a disregard for using data to inform decision-making.

Much of this will permeate from the top, but those brought in to lead on data also play a significant role in how an organization develops a data culture. Where culture meets personal interests, and where ego and ambitions meet data, data can be used responsibly and sensibly, or wielded as a weapon to be utilized only when it meets personal goals or ignored to pursue an ideological agenda.

However, where data cultures are nascent, and there is a willingness to adopt a strong data culture, data leaders can play a significant role in how they influence the data culture in an organization. This ranges from how they communicate and interact with their senior stakeholders, peers and colleagues across the business to how they hire, manage and nurture their data team.

During most of my career I have created, grown and nurtured data teams in almost every organization I have been in. This experience has taught me that not all organizations adopt or practise a healthy data culture, and even where there is a will to do so, if there are not the right conditions then it can be hard. I have also found that if I and other data leaders live the values and beliefs of a healthy data culture, then the teams we build also reflect those values and beliefs in the way they work and interact with the rest of the business, and this then influences how the data culture evolves in an organization.

It is a self-fulfilling prophecy – when the data team and its leader live the values of a good data culture, then the rest of the organization follows that example. It is also true that if the organization at a senior level fosters a healthy data culture, then the data team feels empowered to also behave accordingly. This means that data teams do need to stay impartial within an organization. Taking sides when using data to support agendas can lead to scepticism from within the organization. If this happens, then trust and faith in the data team is not the only thing that is lost – the data is lost as well.

Why organizations do not automatically have a data culture

I wanted to start this book by describing the 'five monkeys' experiment as an example of how organizational culture forms. However, when you have been exposed to a data culture like academia, you instinctively want to find a reference for the experiment. Something that was quite shocking when I left academia and joined the world of work was that references were rarely asked for.

Anyway, for those of you who don't know about the study, it goes something like this.

The 'five monkeys' experiment

An experiment was conducted where five monkeys were placed in a cage with a ladder in the middle of the cage. On top of the ladder were some bananas. Every time a monkey tried to climb the ladder, all of the monkeys were sprayed with icy water by the experimenter. Eventually, the monkeys learnt that climbing the ladder for the bananas was not a good thing and each time a monkey started to climb the ladder, the others pulled him off and beat him up so they could avoid the icy spray. As a result, none of the monkeys climbed the ladder again. This is an example of classical conditioning.

Then one of the original monkeys in the cage was substituted with a new monkey by the experimenters. When this new monkey saw the bananas on top of the ladder, the first thing it tried to do was climb the ladder to reach the banana. However, the other four monkeys knew what was coming, so they pulled the new monkey down and beat it whenever it tried to climb the ladder and get the bananas. After being stopped and beaten several times, the new monkey learned that it was the social norm not to climb the ladder to get the bananas. The monkey never knew why, as he had never been sprayed with ice water, but quickly learnt that this behaviour of climbing the ladder to get the bananas would not be tolerated by the other monkeys.

The experimenters then, one by one, substituted each of the original monkeys in the cage with a new monkey, until the cage contained none of the original five monkeys. Every time a new monkey went up the ladder, the rest of the group pulled him down, even those who had never been sprayed with the icy water.

By the end of the experiment, the five monkeys in the cage, who had never been sprayed with ice water, had learned to follow the rule (don't go for the bananas), without any of them knowing the reason why (we'll all get sprayed by icy water).

It was hypothesized by the experimenters that if they could have asked the monkeys for their rationale behind not letting their cage mates climb the ladder, their answer would probably be: 'I don't know, that's just how it's always been done.'

Now had this study actually occurred, it would have given a classic example of culture and how organizations develop culture through the observation of others already in the organization. But it is probably just a parable used by business coaches to teach a fundamental lesson to people. However, there is one documented study that the five monkeys study is probably based on, which teaches us the lesson that organizational behaviours do not necessarily have to be fixed, just as cultures in societies are not fixed and are dynamic. In this study, 'Cultural acquisition of a specific learned response among rhesus monkeys' (Stephenson, 1967), the researcher placed a monkey in a cage with an item and made them fear it by hitting them with several blasts of air. Once the fear was learned, a naive monkey was placed in the cage. When the naive monkey tried to touch the items, in only one of the four experiments did a scared monkey pull the naive monkey away, whilst in the other three experiments the scared monkeys just looked fearfully at the naive monkey.

The fact that some people believe the 'five monkeys' experiment actually occurred shows that society in general and business specifically do not inherently have a data culture or that it is not necessarily strong. People seem to be happy to propagate information without checking whether it has any factual basis or doing any due diligence to check what evidence there is for the claims being made. This 'five monkeys' experiment is referred to in many business coaching articles, and it is only when I wanted to reference it for this book that I decided to validate whether it was true. Since my personal data culture is heavily influenced by academia, something I talk of later, this seems natural to me. However, speaking with many people I work with or have worked with, this is not the norm.

The dissemination of the 'five monkeys' experiment illustrates why many organizations do not automatically have a data culture, or the one they have may not be particularly strong. If we look at general discussion on social media, people are happy to believe things that seem plausible, without questioning their authenticity or accuracy. I mentioned the 'five monkeys' experiment to a few dozen people in person and through other communication methods, such as WhatsApp, Slack and email, and not one person, including data analysts amongst them, questioned whether the study was true. In my experience, this is also quite pronounced in organizations that I have worked for or engaged with. I've found that individuals, occasionally quite senior and also some who should have an evidence-based background such as a scientific qualification, tend to believe statements or make statements without any data or evidence to back them up. This is even more likely when the statement being made reinforces existing beliefs or views, or just makes logical sense, like the 'five monkeys' experiment, based on an individual's pre-existing perceptions of the world.

What is culture, and specifically data culture?

Culture is considered a central concept in anthropology, encompassing the range of phenomena that are transmitted through social learning in human societies. A culture is a way of life of a group of people – the behaviours, beliefs, values and symbols that they accept, generally without thinking about them, and that are passed along by communication and imitation from one generation to the next.

We all have a culture or adapt to many. We have an ethnic culture which we learn from our friends and family, and some of us have a religious culture which is taught through scripture and practices. We also have a national culture, one that we learn through formal and informal instruction on how to behave, that reflects what we believe and the values to hold when living in certain nations. There is also a work culture, something we learn by osmosis through observation, feedback and interaction with others in the workplace.

The thing to note here is that there is no uniformity or consensus in how any of these cultures manifest themselves. People may behave differently or hold very different values though they are from the same nation, or have very different practices but claim to share the same religious or ethnic culture. Data culture is no different. It is a set of beliefs, values and practices which are shared amongst people when they are in a common collection such as a company. Therefore, though you may see people behave differently, they will hold core values and beliefs about using data to inform decision-making or to support a viewpoint or argument, but the manifested behaviours may be different.

You may find that a group or person may only be convinced if they have all the data available, but another group may be happy to make a decision with incomplete data and be willing to make a start and not search for further data to support or challenge their decision. Some individuals will combine data with experience, which in itself is a collation of data points, whereas some will evaluate how others interpret the data and then make a decision based on a consensus view of the truth.

Data culture in organizations will manifest itself through the way people use data; many organizations will share a vision of being data-driven, or allied terms like customer-centric, which implies looking at data to understand the customer better, or even have bold statements such as using data to infuse creativity. How this is practised by the organization as a whole, or by different teams, can and will vary.

My experience has been that this comes down to how those who influence the data culture in an organization, typically senior leadership including data leaders, have themselves learnt what data culture means.

How I developed my data culture

Working with data is not a new phenomenon in society or business in general. Therefore, individuals in organizations should have some idea of what a healthy and positive data culture looks like, especially those who have undertaken higher education, where they may have been required to conduct experiments. The basis of empirical research requires the collection of evidence and data, to substantiate a hypothesis.

When I was studying psychology at university for my undergraduate and master's degree, and later for my PhD, I was collecting data for my theses and dissertations. As a psychology student, it was natural for me to understand that you couldn't just make a statement about something without having evidence, or data, to back up that claim, a position that was made more acute when I was doing my PhD. I recall when my supervisor would review my thesis periodically and ask where my reference for this piece of information was or why I believed this, or what led me to this conclusion. She would always ask what *evidence* I had to support my hypothesis.

In general, in academia, I found that opinions and views were substantiated with facts and figures. Very rarely did we have debates or do a presentation where we expressed a point of view without backing it up with some data from a study. It was true that the interpretation could be subjective, but at least that interpretation was based on something factual and objective, which others had access to and could provide their own interpretation but not reinvention of the facts.

When I finished my PhD I decided that I wanted to apply my qualifications in a 'real world' setting, in the area of health promotion and preventing ill health. I applied for roles with the NHS and was offered a post in my desired field. Before starting, I assumed that the data culture of universities would permeate the workplace, especially in the NHS. Working with physicians, one would expect a level of scientific rigour in their approach; however, when designing experiments or interventions in the hospital setting around promoting well-being, I found that the data culture in hospitals was less rigorous than in academia.

For example, I was assisting a consultant to run an experiment in the ambulatory care unit to evaluate the effectiveness of using story-telling to alleviate the anxiety of children undergoing ultrasounds and x-rays. I was surprised that the questionnaire designed to measure anxiety in children pre- and post- the story being told was not validated with a pilot or that a test–retest reliability study was not done to ensure the accuracy and validity of the questions, and then finally that the data collected was analysed by just looking at the mean scores, not understanding whether the difference in the mean scores was significant by using a t-test. Raising these issues, I reasoned that these interventions were not for academic purposes, even though the ambition was to publish them, but that the results were to be used to show whether these interventions worked or not. In this instance, the results did not support the hypothesis, but in my opinion this was owing more to a poorly run experiment than to the hypothesis itself.

This experience highlighted to me that the robust and high data standards of academia are not universally practised, and so the data culture I had developed and practised was probably at the more extreme end. It was an interesting experience, and one of many, as I reconciled getting things done with getting things done the way I thought they should be done.

Later, I would learn that what I had experienced in the NHS was much better than what I saw in local government, where I ran several studies using Neighbourhood Renewal Funding and found that descriptive statistics were sufficient for most purposes to prove if something worked or not, and sometimes even these were not presented, just counts of activity, such as how many people did something and how many did not. When I tried to introduce some statistical rigour, I was met with some hostility from certain areas, something at the time I found quite uncomfortable. Later, I learnt to get used to it, as

I found it was a common reaction when data was used objectively. My early experience reflects what I still see today. In my discussion with many data leaders, I witness that the objective of many parts of businesses is to just achieve a key performance indicator (KPI), and those involved are happy even to change definitions to achieve a specific objective.

A particular episode sticks in my mind. Very early when working in local government during a workshop, a lead for one of the projects attacked me for being too robust, and said that it was slowing down what they wanted to achieve. That episode also taught me about the 'people' component of data culture, whereby, unless people have shared values, you will be misaligned on what you are trying to achieve. I was trying to measure and evaluate things robustly and in a way that I thought was correct, but my peers wanted to just measure things to hit a target.

Later in my experience working in the private sector, I learnt that aligning with stakeholder expectations is as important as doing the analysis. If your stakeholders are not bought into what you are doing, the analysis and how you are doing it, then it doesn't matter what the output is – unless it contributes to meeting their goals, the data and its corresponding analysis and insight will be ignored. However, if you can work with your stakeholders to align them to what analysis you are doing and why, you can actually influence how the data and its findings are used by your stakeholders within the organization. Even though you may not be able to practise data culture to the standards of academia, you can avoid scenarios where data is totally ignored.

The other thing I learned about data cultures in the private sector is that good enough is good enough. In one of my early roles I built propensity models for the marketing team, and I spent a significant amount of time tweaking my models from being 80 per cent accurate to just over 90 per cent. These extra percentage points in accuracy would take a disproportionate amount of time, whereas the business was happy with the 80 per cent model, and the extra time I spent improving the accuracy of the model was not valued.

Organizations need to balance the need for understanding what the data is telling them, and how quickly it can tell them that, with the practicalities of getting things done. This balance determines the type of data culture an organization develops. I have observed this balance and it has influenced how I use data in the different roles I have occupied. For me, that balance was hard, and still is, especially when you spend a significant amount of your formative adult years absorbing the data culture of academia. Without being purists, I have noticed amongst my peer group of other data leaders that there is a subset who also feel like me – that data is not always being used as well as it should be.

Defining data culture

There is no agreement on what a data culture is. However, a simple search online will come up with many definitions, but with a common theme that data culture is the collective behaviours and beliefs of people within an organization who value, practise and encourage the use of data to improve decision-making.

Like other cultures, there is a spectrum in how people practise a data culture. There will be people who are good examples and representations of the data culture, and there will be people who are bad examples. Also, like other cultures, there will be people who are extreme on either side. For example, some people don't make a decision without having all the data, and a sense of decision paralysis emerges as they are always waiting for that extra bit of data, whereas people at the other extreme ignore all the facts and make a decision based on what serves their best interest. Being in the middle, good or bad, is probably where an organization wants its people to be.

Therefore, organizations with a healthy data culture will find that their people's beliefs and values about being data-driven are close to the organization's. They may not be perfect, but they will be close enough that as an organization they all share the same grounding when making a decision, especially one that requires the business to change direction or stay on course.

Data culture requires the shared belief that the numbers used by the business are correct or as accurate as they can be, and that even with incomplete data or some quality issues, the business can move forward by basing their decisions on the best available information. When conflicting numbers arise owing to different data sources being used, for example customer acquisition numbers based on internal tools and third-party marketing technology tools which will naturally differ, the organization needs to agree on a single source of truth. Just using numbers is not enough to have a good data culture, there also needs to be consensus on what data source to use for each metric and KPI that the business reports on.

Companies with a good data culture will exhibit this through centralizing or unifying their data, having good data governance and agreeing upon the single source of truth for all their KPIs and metrics.

Data culture is part of business culture

We don't go around making things up. Even though we are going through a period where misinformation is prominent and the widespread use of social media has allowed it to be propagated, most people know when something is based on evidence, i.e. the truth, and something that is not based on any facts, i.e. lies.

However, it is not so clear cut. Just as there are many variations in a culture, there are also many different variations of data culture. No one version of the culture is better than the other and societies have developed variations of these cultures in line with what works for them. This means that, in some cultures, the data culture relies less on observed evidence and more on experiential evidence. For example, in agricultural communities, knowledge from older people is typically given more weight than those from younger people who may have a formal education in agriculture. These societies have evolved their culture to give more value to the people who have done the activity than those that have 'learnt' about it. The elders are especially respected as the repositories of inherited wisdom and experience passed down orally from one generation to the next (Helman, 2005).

In other cultures, such as academia, we value experts, whose opinions are based on the history of scientific experimentation and rational arguments. Here data culture will be given more value. As mentioned, that is where I developed my version of a data culture. In our technological culture we give value to software engineers who can build solutions to some of the world's pressing problems.

Businesses, however, have a natural culture of using numbers to measure financial performance. Organizations spend a lot of time, resources and money reporting how they are performing financially. This information is shared in different levels of detail to a variety of audiences, and organizations listed on stock markets ensure that the numbers they produce can be audited and validated. Financial reports also need to follow a common methodology, so that those in the accounting and finance space interpret the numbers in a similar way, whether that is to make investment, valuation or sustainability decisions.

But, beyond financial reporting, some companies may also be very data-driven, such as banks who deal with a lot of data, whereas others rely more on experience and creativity, such as advertising agencies. But both will have some form of data culture, whether that be to report on company finances, advertising effectiveness, customer satisfaction, average revenue per user, etc. How that culture manifests itself will depend on the people who lead and set the agenda on the use of data.

This then means that, to develop a healthy data culture, organizations must be seen to do it as well as believe in it. It is not enough just to make bold statements or put out visions and goals about using data; the people in the organization must be seen to do this as well as believe in it.

Therefore, just talking about being data-driven or using data to make decisions is not enough. Senior leaders need to practise this. This involves being overt about referring to data when making decisions. Too often, senior leaders will make decisions and announce them to the whole organization without context, especially how they came to that decision. A company that has data culture as part of its company culture will talk about the company's performance in terms of data points, such as sales, customer numbers, average revenue per user or profitability, and why this has led them to certain decisions.

Data culture cannot be seen as something separate that is developed outside the business. It needs to be embedded in the business and be part of the company's vision and values. Companies, however, know this – if you speak to any senior leader they will tell you how important data is to their organization, and many clients I speak with emphasize how they want to be data-driven so they can utilize the latest in artificial intelligence (AI) technologies.

So, if data is seen as a strategic asset, why are organizations not using it to its full capacity? In my discussions for the book and generally with other data leaders, we all acknowledge that there is so much more companies could do with data, but there seems to be a reluctance to fully embrace this. There is this fear that letting data out of the box means that the company will somehow lose control. To be data-driven or to be able to use applications such as machine learning (ML) and AI, companies need to believe that utilizing data can help them achieve that, and their company values must also reflect this.

Having worked in the data space in some form or other for over two decades, I have encountered many companies who claim to want to be data-driven or want to use data so they can deliver better experiences or leverage the latest in ML and AI to make their company more efficient and innovative. However, this does not always translate into practice, and one of the main reasons is that it's harder to spot a bad data culture than notice a good one. Good data cultures are those where you immediately get the sense that the organization wants to do what's best with the data they have. Bad data culture is harder to spot, as often it's not something specific about the company culture that is bad, but rather one of many things that are bad within the culture of the company.

That makes isolating a bad data culture within a bad or toxic company culture harder, as rarely do I see just a bad data culture within a very good company culture. For example, in some marketing or digital agencies where data is supposed to be key to creating a great offering, often the people culture in the organization is not conducive to having a good data culture. This often manifests itself as the data team being a service delivery unit, just waiting to be briefed on data requests and rarely being asked to contribute to the wider business strategy or even given direct access to clients to clarify what data and analysis they need. This setup of the data team being subservient to other teams within the agency, for example strategy or account management, limits the capability of the data team and even restricts their ability to deliver great work. The data team then feels demoralized and this impacts the way they work, which in turn can lead to frustration by the wider agency that they are not delivering what is needed by the client. The combination of factors means that even with the will to want to use data to deliver great work, the wider organizational culture negatively impacts this ambition.

Therefore, data culture has to be integrated into the wider company culture for it to have any significant impact on current and future organizational practices. It's not just something preached by senior leadership, or data analytical skills exhibited by data experts; it's not even that the right technologies have been deployed and the correct governance is in place. Rather, data culture is a collection of all of those things and more. Data culture is when the people within the organization hold the belief and behave in line with that belief that to make an informed decision they must evaluate all the evidence in an objective way, and respect the people who do this work. This then needs to be coupled with the organization investing in the technology and processes to allow the practice of being data-driven to become a reality.

A way to work together

So, why the need for a healthy or good data culture in any organization? Does it matter if an organization has a poor data culture or even a weak one? Even those that do have a weak or poor data culture seem to function and it's not the sole reason for success for all companies. In the next chapter I will explore further the importance of having a data culture. However, to conclude this chapter it is worth picking up on this theme. Companies have always been using data, even if it is just for financial reporting, so a nascent or underlying data culture should exist in most companies.

But in today's modern business environment data is an essential component of growth, competitive advantage and survival. This may be a bold statement, but unless individuals within an organization have common ground from which to formulate strategies and plan then it's hard to start, and later it is hard to move forward without being able to evaluate whether the plan or strategy is working. Therefore, data becomes a common language from which to work together. It should provide an objective foundation from which to understand how your business is performing to formulate strategies and plans, and then monitor that data to understand how you are performing after executing your strategy or plans.

Working on a foundation of facts allows healthy debate. If a senior executive decides that the facts do not matter and that they know best, which does happen, then organizations often find themselves suffering from the effects of badly thought-out and executed decisions. Whereas, if everyone agrees that the data provides an objective view about where the business is, and how they want to move forward, then this common language of data provides that basis.

By basing decisions on data, the whole organization can at least understand the rationale for the decision and not have to be convinced by a persuasive orator of their idea. This provides for a healthier debate around decisions and ideas that can be supported or not based on facts. Though it is not necessary for every decision to be wholly reliant on data, the starting point must be some factual evidence so that, when debating the issue, individuals can relate to the common denominator.

The need to utilize data

An aspect of having a good data culture is the utilization of that data. I spoke with a number of data leaders when writing this book, and one of them, Stephen Kinsella, Director, Analytics and Technologies at dmg media made, a particularly apt comment. He pointed out that without a data culture data will not be leveraged. It is tempting to collect data on the assumption that you will use it and drive value from it. This is analogous to buying a gym membership in the hope that you will go to the gym and get fit. It doesn't always work out that way. In Chapter 3 I explain in more detail why hiring analysts and buying data technology is not enough to have a data culture. These are only enablers, and collecting data, buying technology that can store and process it and having people to analyse it is not enough if you don't actually utilize the data.

Companies will try to take the first step to being data-driven, hoping that building a data culture can be accelerated by just putting things in place. Beyond the people, technology and process, the organization needs to see data as an asset that needs to be utilized. An asset if used well can help them gain a competitive advantage, grow and even provide new revenue streams. Just as digitization of an organization results in implementing technologies which make existing processes, procedures and working practices more efficient, thereby making an organization more effective, the value can only truly be realized if the benefits of digitization are utilized.

For example, there is no point in implementing an enterprise resource planning (ERP) system if different teams decide to store documentation, processes and knowledge locally on individuals' personal computers. Data needs to be utilized in the same way to be effective, and to do that an organization with a data culture will recognize the need to embed the use of data into its day-to-day practices.

This requires a change in how people across the organization engage not only with data, but also with the people who conduct the analysis, and how they work with the data tools available and do not misuse them. It also requires processes to be put in place, both top-down and bottom-up, that allow data teams to be effectively integrated into business operations and different teams to work easily with data.

There is also a need for data to be democratized in both its use and ownership. Only then can organizations utilize data that is fit for purpose. This will mean embarking on improving the data literacy of the organization. This may be via formal training as well as via informal interaction with data forums which allow a safe space for people to ask questions of the data, including what it means and how it's collected. Finally, organizations can only maintain a healthy data culture if senior leaders are seen to be data-driven. This not only means that they value the data itself, but also they value the people and teams who deliver the data and analysis.

In the rest of this book I will explore why it is important to establish a data culture, how you should start and what to avoid. I will draw upon my personal experience of building data teams and, in discussion with other senior data leaders, explore how to build and nurture a data team. Then I will look at how you know when your organization has a healthy data culture – what the signs are that indicate a healthy data culture. Finally, I will explore how you maintain and measure the health of an organization's data culture, and what can be achieved when you have a good data culture.

References

Helman, C G (2005) *Cultural Aspects of Time and Ageing*, European Molecular Biology Organization, Heidelberg

Pavlov, I P (1927) *Conditioned Reflexes: An investigation of the physiological activity of the cerebral cortex*, Oxford University Press, Oxford

Stephenson, G R (1967) Cultural acquisition of a specific learned response among rhesus monkeys, in D Stark, R Schneider and H J Kuhn, 279–88, *Progress in Primatology*, Gustav Fischer Verlag, Stuttgart

Why is it important to establish a data culture in your organization?

2

When I ask clients I have engaged with what they need data for, the most common answer is that they want to be data-driven. This is something that they know they must do and they acknowledge that, to be data-driven, they need to make the best use of data. Even amongst data leaders there is a consensus that most companies want to be data-driven. So, what would a data-driven organization look like? Well, for a start, it has integrated data analysis into the core of its business processes, including when making tactical and strategic decisions. Companies then use the insights they get from this analysis to transform business processes.

Data-driven organizations have a key focus on driving efficiencies, ensuring automation where possible, continual improvement and optimization (test and learn), and the ability to anticipate internal and external changes. Most of all, they should have an organizational culture that fully embraces data and its potential. When speaking with Julie Screech, an independent data strategy and tech consultant who has served as a data lead for many major brands, she made an interesting point that being data-driven is having a data culture that sets the prerequisite for an organization and its people to be curious about things – to have an inquisitive and experimental mindset.

What she later went on to explain was that having a good and healthy data culture allows the organization to build a healthy balance of asking questions and the courage to test things when they don't know the answer. This aligned to my early experience of a data culture, primarily in academia, where individuals were comfortable asking questions and challenging ideas, and then running experiments when they did not know the answer or to find out new things.

A data culture provides a framework from which organizations can learn new things and move forward confidently, knowing that their decisions are based on facts. It also means that they are adaptable to learning, that what they knew yesterday could change today as new data comes in, and may also change tomorrow as they collect and analyse further data.

As I put it to a marketing director once when we were testing a recommendation engine, we need to refresh the model periodically, because what we know about what customers are likely to buy next through the current recommendations will become obsolete when they actually buy the item, and the model will need to be adapted to accommodate this new information. In essence, when you try to impact a customer's experience and are successful, that results in a new data point which changes what they will do in the future.

The explosion of data

Unless you have been hiding in a cave, data is now the 'next big thing'. Some have referred to data as the new oil, especially in the context of the digital economy. Exploding quantities of data have the potential to fuel a new era of fact-based innovation in companies, backing up new ideas with solid evidence.

With the internet, we have the potential and capability to collect petabytes of data. Every interaction a person makes with a digital asset creates data, and the interaction between systems, especially in the realm of the Internet of Things (IoT), also generates data. It is now possible to collect all this data, store it cheaply and analyse it with the distributed cloud computing power that we can use at will.

One would expect that, with access to such vast oceans of data, decision-making would rely more on data rather than less. A poignant point that Stephen Kinsella made in my discussion with him is that he believes all companies are now also data companies, and he can't see how any modern business could operate without data. He went on to discuss how, with many companies digitizing their offerings, they were in fact casting a net out to capture more and more data. At some point he believes some companies can create products off the back of data that can make more money than traditional products.

However, where opportunities for companies to use data well have grown, there are also opportunities for some companies to use data badly. Sometimes this is not deliberate, but when an organization has not agreed upon a common set of values, beliefs and behaviours around data, it becomes all too easy to 'have your own data'.

With the explosion of data, collecting it is cheap and therefore everyone is doing it. In the past, if you wanted to understand how your advertising or marketing was performing, you would typically rely on one or maybe two sources of information. For example, the Broadcasters' Audience Research Board (BARB) used to be the only source of information for measuring and understanding advertising viewed on TV. Now, adverts streamed into video on demand (VoD) content can be tracked and there are several sources collecting that information. For example, the tracking technology within the VoD player, the advert server, a data management platform (DMP), and a host of other third-party advert effectiveness or optimization technologies could also be tracking this information and collecting data.

Though this should be a good thing, as many sources can help you to understand what the 'real' truth is, if there is no healthy data culture it becomes too easy for different teams and departments to create their own siloed data empires, and instead of sharing and learning from each other to use data selectively to provide evidence of the success of their activity.

A common issue is that the data team reports on different metrics to, say, the marketing or finance teams. This happens because the marketing team may have access to data from a marketing system that the data team does not or cannot have access to. A typical example is Facebook ads or Google Ads data versus an organization's internal digital analytics data, when trying to calculate say something like attribution by marketing channel.

Marketing teams will come to meetings with data from Facebook Ads or Google Ads, stating that the number of referrals, conversions or acquisitions is higher than that reported by the organization's digital analytics tool via the data team. The data team will state that the digital analytics tool is accurately collecting data and that all marketing channel data is also accurately captured. However, even with all this due diligence the numbers will not match, the primary reason being that attribution data provided by marketing platforms such as Facebook and Google Ads will report on data that is not captured by the data team's tools. For example, when someone sees an ad on Facebook but then instead of clicking on the ad decides to visit the website either directly or by searching on Google, the Facebook pixel will be able to track this individual across Facebook and the organization's website, but the organization's internal digital analytics tool will not be able to track that this person had seen an ad in Facebook. This then leads to discrepancies in the data and conflict between the data team and respective departments about which numbers are the true and accurate numbers.

Also, with the ability to also store and process data cheaply using cloud technology platforms, or even third-party hosted solutions, there has been a proliferation of not only data but also data teams. A recent discussion with a data leader revealed that a certain part of their business was not hitting its targets, with numbers being independently provided by his team to the board. Instead of speaking with the data team and learning why they were not hitting their targets, they have instead made a case to the business to hire their own analysts who will be closer to their area of business and therefore provide more context to the numbers, a subtext to allow them to preview and where possible manipulate the numbers to provide an alternative view to the board of their performance.

Unfortunately, this is not an isolated incident. I have worked with several clients where some departments have made the case to have their own analyst or even teams of analysts, for whatever reason, and instead of being more data-driven they seem less, with too much data and analysis providing competing and contradictory information. The senior leadership are then confused as to what to believe, leading them to distrust all information.

The explosion of data should have made building a data culture easier, with more and more data being available to an organization to understand its business, customers and products better, but it also has the potential to create its own problems by allowing different departments and teams to have their own versions of the truth. Though this is not a bad thing, as more data from different perspectives can enrich the information and knowledge that a company analyses, this can only happen if the underlying data culture is nurtured, in different departments and teams, to work towards a common goal. Part of that is also understanding how the data is analysed and reported on by the internal data team and also by external third parties which companies rely on for different data sets. With software-as-a-service (SaaS) applications, people do not always have access to the raw data that is collected on their behalf by these systems and so they must rely on the third-party vendor to be trustworthy when providing them with analysis and insights.

Having trust and faith in your data team will allow the organization to ask for their expert opinion. However, sometimes the data team does not simplify the complex data, and this can lead to opinions and advice not being sought.

The rise of data science, machine learning and artificial intelligence

One of the reasons that some data teams find it difficult to explain or simplify analysis from third parties or even analysis that they have done is the frequent adoption of new technologies and methodologies in data analytics which allow someone with a basic understanding of a programming language such as Python to run extremely complex ML algorithms.

In the hands of third-party vendors, these tools have resulted in them floating terms like AI and stating how their product uses AI to do such-and-such, when often the product is merely using advanced statistical analysis to come up with a metric of KPI in an obscure and 'black box' way. This means that no one is quite sure how different metrics and KPIs are calculated. Imagine a SaaS solution that aims to predict the likelihood of a user converting or subscribing, and claims to use AI to calculate this score. It then hides behind proprietary intellectual property arguments for not revealing the methodology. This then makes it hard for internal data teams or even others to evaluate the claims these tools make objectively.

Teams such as marketing, sales or product might procure these tools and report on propensity scores increasing without anyone in the organization understanding what that means. They then look at internal hard data like subscriptions or sales and note that the increase in propensity scores has not resulted in the same increase in subscription or sales. Teams then get into a debate (or more often an argument) about why this is, claiming that the software development team haven't improved checkout experience speed, which is why customers are not converting, or that the commercial team haven't improved the offers they give prospective customers that will make them subscribers, or that the content team are not creating compelling content. Not once is the propensity score questioned, not even whether it is actually reporting on what is being claimed.

The art of data science, leveraging data and algorithms to provide companies with insights and applications of knowledge has transformed how companies see data. Moving away from just looking backwards at what has happened, they can now utilize the latest in convoluted neural networks, decision trees and predictive analytics to look forward, and confidently anticipate future performance.

The hype surrounding this area, from Amazon's recommendation engine to Open AI's ChatGPT, has got organizations envisioning possibilities that may have once seemed like science fiction. The marketing surrounding data science, ML and AI suggests that any company can do it. They just need to hire the right people or consultancy and the right technology and they would have access to the latest in data tech to revolutionize their business. This has led to companies hiring resources, and acquiring technology, only to later realize that they are several steps behind where they need to be in order to leverage anything close to AI or even machine learning.

A common reason for this is that these companies have not fully understood what it takes to make these models work, from collecting the right data, to ensuring that it is of high quality and that it is accessible in a unified repository for these ML and AI applications to be able to ingest, process, analyse and execute, to having the systems in place that make moving data across systems seamless. A well-established data culture that promotes data at the heart of the organization is required to leverage the advanced end of data applications,

Data culture as an enabler

Though I would argue that all organizations should, to some extent, have a data culture already as part of their organizational culture, it is not always evident. In theory, as individuals we operate in a wider society where we try to make rational and logical decisions based on the information we are presented with. However, we know in reality that this is not the case. People don't always make logical decisions; they often go with what feels right.

In *Thinking, Fast and Slow* (2011), Daniel Kahneman, the renowned psychologist, explains that the way we make decisions is based on two systems. One system is fast, intuitive and emotional; the other is slower, more deliberative and more logical. Though system one allows us to make decisions really quickly, based on what we might call intuition, it comes with faults and biases and Kahneman exposes the pervasive influence of intuitive impressions on our thoughts and behaviours. System two is slow, deliberate and more logical, and we use it when we need to think deeply about a decision. System two takes more energy and effort and the individual is often left with the difficult task of evaluating the evidence and making a decision. In organizations, and society in general, we get information typically from other people and rarely from the primary source, and how that information is presented, framed and delivered has a huge impact on how we receive it, and ultimately whether we believe it.

Where information is presented in a convincing format by a great orator, we may find that system one kicks into play when making a decision, as your intuition tells you to trust what is being said, and if it is delivered by someone who you believe has the authority to do so, you are more likely to believe it. In these situations, you are less likely to question what you are hearing and think logically about the information being presented. This approach then makes it easier for someone to convince senior stakeholders in organizations to go ahead with their ideas and recommendation not based on the actual facts or data that is presented but on how they chose to deliver and position that information.

Where businesses are being exposed to the ever-growing deluge of data, using data badly or not at all to convince others of your position is getting easier. Therefore, establishing a healthy data culture allows organizations to use data systematically and universally across the entire organization. A data culture can also avoid many of the pitfalls when a company starts to use data in earnest, from lack of bandwidth in the data team to deliver everything that is needed, to departments and teams creating separated and siloed data teams and systems.

A healthy data culture also becomes an enabler for many other things, from ensuring that all parts of the business know why they need to collect good quality data, and storing that data in platforms that allows it to be easily and accurately retrieved, to developing good governance that allows the data to be tagged, labelled and categorized according to business needs, and reporting that information in a timely manner with insights that the business can use. This makes moving forward with more advanced use cases so much easier as the foundations are in place.

However, for data culture to be truly an enabler, everyone in the organization needs to understand the role they play in that culture. This ranges from software developers who create applications that collect data, to customer support teams who capture customer feedback, to marketing and content teams who need to label campaigns and content consistently and robustly.

When working with teams who don't think that the data they collect has any importance anywhere in the business I have often demonstrated, for example, that if customer services staff collect good quality data from customer calls and emails, instead of just leaving fields blank and ticking default options to allow them to close a case, the data they collect can enable the data scientist to help the business understand why people are calling, what the business can do about it and also empower the customer service staff with tools and aids that can help them deal with customer interactions better.

Or I have explained to marketing teams that if they label their digital marketing campaigns more carefully, instead of just copying and pasting from past campaigns, this will allow the data team to analyse in far more granularity and accuracy what campaigns work and which ones do not, and potentially why, through natural language processing (NLP) and computer vision applications. This then allows the marketing team to take that insight to plan future campaigns with learning from the past, to continually improve and create more effective marketing campaigns. This need to use data for decision-making and continually learn and adapt is enabled with a good data culture.

Data-driven and data-informed

The reality, though, is that no one is expecting that every decision made by individuals in organizations should be dictated by data; rather, these decisions should be data-driven or data-informed. This means that decisions taken should be based on some evidence that allows others to understand why that decision was made in the first place.

Why this is important is that, as you will find if you look at any evidence-based domain such as academia or medicine, basing decisions, judgements, views or opinions on an evidence base allows a common framework for alignment between individuals within and across organizations. So, when you state that you want to create a marketing campaign that is more emotional than rational, you can point to a study by Les Binet and Peter Field (2013) which found that rational strategies, while delivering quick results, are, for the most part, not memorable. Over the long term, it is emotional advertising that will deliver long-term success, build brand fame and drive price elasticity and therefore profit. Using this evidence to make a more emotional advert is an example of being data-driven or data-informed.

In a recent experience with a client, they wanted to change their product from a freemium model (free to use initially and then requiring a subscription to access premium content) to a purely subscription based one. Their rationale was that when looking at their data, most people who started on the free version rarely upgraded, whereas those that paid for a subscription generally tended to renew and stay engaged with the product. We could see from the data that it seemed that the free version was bringing people with low interest from the paid marketing that was done, whereas those that subscribed straight away were using the service regularly. Based on this information, it made sense to stop a free version, this meant they would save money and effort which could be directed to the paid parts behind the subscription wall, and also the marketing budget could then be wholly focused on acquiring paying customers.

So, even though the data didn't tell them that this was the right thing to do, it informed their decision to go ahead with an idea they were thinking about. By basing decisions on data, people can come to an agreement on what direction to go forward with. That is not to say that everyone will interpret the data in the same way; obviously, biases and prejudices will influence how the data is interpreted, but at a base level there will be some fundamental truths that will drive a common language.

What this means is that by being data-driven people can agree that the data itself, irrespective of how it is interpreted, is the truth. This is fundamental, as, if there are many versions of the truth, or if the truth is not widely accepted, then you do not have a basis for a data culture. Therefore, a healthy data culture will instil in the company not only what they do, but also what data they base their decisions on.

Retained wisdom

Those in the business intelligence space will be familiar with the data, information, knowledge and wisdom pyramid (Figure 2.1). It is a common model used to explain how data operates at different stages and where businesses typically operate.

Figure 2.1 Data–information–knowledge–wisdom pyramid

The pyramid shows how we extract information from data and then the information is transformed into knowledge and finally that knowledge becomes wisdom. However, often if you stay in a company for long enough, and see changes at the top a few times, you will notice that the same mistakes are made. It is as if knowledge learnt from previous experiences has been forgotten. A big part of this is because the knowledge within an organization is not retained as wisdom.

That wisdom doesn't become part of a company's DNA and, eventually, knowledge about what worked or didn't work is forgotten, and the information that led to that knowledge, often represented in PowerPoint slides, is buried deep in folders on company servers. The data may still be there, waiting to be reanalysed once the mistakes have already been repeated.

Retained wisdom within an organization is an interesting concept. Just like humans, organizations can retain wisdom, taking a multitude of knowledge and converting that into wisdom to advise and guide the next generation not to make the same mistakes we made. If we think about how we pass on information, we typically socialize it. When explaining to children why they shouldn't cross the road without looking, we use different strategies from educating, to instilling fear, to showing by doing. This ensures that knowledge is transmitted naturally to others, who in turn then pass that knowledge to others.

Another method of transmitting wisdom is storytelling, whether written, orally or theatrically. We have developed cultural practices which allow us to retain wisdom within communities and societies by passing our knowledge to others in various forms. Therefore, embedded in the organization's data culture needs to be practices which ensure that wisdom is retained, and that there are mechanisms to pass down knowledge to others that are part of an organization's general culture.

However, to retain wisdom, especially when deciding what to do next, a company needs to have a data culture that allows new ideas to be evaluated through the lens of what a company already knows. This cannot be dependent on a single person, but must be stored in the collective mind of the organization. Where a company has a healthy data culture, you will find that the right questions will be asked when new ideas are proposed, knowledge of what has worked in the past will be sought and critical evaluation of opinions will occur.

This practice ensures the continuation of knowledge, so that it becomes retained wisdom within the organization, and though not everything that has been learnt is retained, the essence of what was learnt is retained, ensuring that similar mistakes are not repeated. I compare this to the literature searches I have done when writing my thesis at university. Though not as rigorous, it allows historical knowledge to be searched systematically to assess what previous research studies have found.

Since most organizations don't have the robust library systems of universities, results of findings can live within various documentation, many of which will not be systematically stored, and definitely not catalogued. Therefore, that knowledge needs to live within the organization in some form. The best way to do that is through the passing of wisdom through individuals as they join the organization. Like the alternative 'five monkeys' experiment, here individuals would know what to do, even though they may not know why.

A common method to retain wisdom by organizations is to create a playbook, guide or cheat sheet. This allows the essence of what has worked in the past and what has not to be captured succinctly so that it triggers the right thought processes in people who join the organization. Other methods include regular presentation of results, creating a culture of data-sharing, and a safe place to ask questions. In Chapter 7 I explore a strategy for this which has worked well for me.

Therefore, asking the right questions, being curious as to why things are done in the way they are, ensuring the right people are involved, particularly the data team, reading some core documentation and even speaking with the wider organization will ensure that the essence of information and knowledge that has become retained wisdom in an organization is revealed and passed on to others. This will allow for objective evaluation of new ideas through the lens of the organization's collective retained wisdom, without an individual feeling that what they are proposing may be wrong or a bad idea.

A common language

The reason I wanted to discuss the concept of retained wisdom is because when an organization starts to develop a healthy data culture, discussing, evaluating and asking questions becomes a normal part of a wider company culture. This openness means that people can have a healthy debate around new and innovative ideas that they may want to test or deploy. For them to do that they need to make sure that the rest of the business understands where they are coming from.

As mentioned in my introduction, data provides organizations with a common language in which to move forward. A common language using data is about agreeing on what KPIs and metrics mean, how to measure success, what 'good' looks like and agreeing when things are going well or badly. By basing decisions on data, a business is able to go across departments with the same understanding of what it wants to achieve. This common language means that, when discussing changes or introducing new ideas, why the change or idea is being proposed should be obvious as a good data culture will always have the individual or team starting off describing what has worked and what hasn't worked in the past, what they have learnt from the data and why they are planning to make the change.

I caught up with Fayez Shriwardhankar, Head of Data at Raconteur, when writing this book and he proposed that part of this common language is that individuals or teams will show a willingness to learn and also recognize that there is more to understand and learn. This shows others in the business that they acknowledge that the data to date is making them consider this change, but later as they learn more from this change and new data, they are willing to consider alternative ideas and views, as they recognize there is still much more to learn. What they are implicitly saying is that they are not emotionally invested in this idea or suggestion, but that their recommendation is based on facts, on data.

Julie gave a good analogy to this common language challenge, which is the parable of the blind men and an elephant (Saxe and Galdone, 1963). It is a story of a group of blind men who have never come across an elephant before and who learn about and imagine what the elephant is like by touching it. Each blind man feels a different part of the elephant's body, but only one part, such as the side or the tusk. They then describe the elephant based on their limited experience, and their descriptions of the elephant are different from each other. The moral of the parable is that humans have a tendency to claim absolute truth based on their limited, subjective experience as they ignore other people's limited, subjective experiences, which may be equally true.

Therefore, as we explore in this book, a data culture requires shared values, beliefs, behaviours and practices. Where the organization is unsure what these should be, then a starting point is the data leader and data team. From my experience, I brought my data culture of academia firstly into the NHS and later into the private and commercial sector, including my own companies. However, along that journey I realized that my interpretation and my position about what a data culture is, was probably somewhat on the extreme side. But though I did allow myself to be slightly flexible to become more centrist, I was always more extreme than my peers.

Finding a balance is important in any organization, as everyone needs to know that decisions and actions taken are based on something that can be understood now, but also evaluated later. This makes it vital for organizations to establish a collective data culture, and although there will be differing opinions about it, the core beliefs and values of adhering to data to establish facts and measure success and outcomes, including understanding how and when data should be used, are important.

This is not something that comes easily to most people. When speaking with Stephen Kinsella we discussed how in our experience a decision has usually been made by someone, and the data team is called upon to support that idea. This is not a symptom of a specific sector or function within a company, but our experience suggests that it is a common occurrence across many organizations. Because of this, there is not a common language used across the business in regard to data and so it becomes hard for a good and healthy data culture to emerge.

All of the data leaders I discussed this particular theme with agreed that, unless the organization's culture can easily accommodate a healthy data culture, data culture is confined to either just the data team or certain teams and functions, with others believing that data does not apply to them.

However, if a company can promote data culture as a common language, it provides for an organization to function well. It ensures that success and failure are to some extent objective and how to move forward is agreed upon.

Changing the way businesses operate

Lara Izlan, Director of Insights and Analytics at ITV, discussed why it's important to establish a data culture in an organization. She mentioned that a company that wants to overtly change, for example, a digital or wider transformation, can use data as an envelope for that change. One of the many catalysts for a wider transformation within the businesses is developing a data culture. Especially if there was an urgency to make that change, they can build a new culture and mindset through the data and the data team. It is an effective way to influence the organization.

But this only works if there is strong data leadership, and a willingness to work within the confines of the existing company culture and build slowly and gradually. It is hard to change organizations. People will tell you 'This is how it has always been done.' I recall having a discussion with a very senior strategist at an advertising agency about how to change the way agencies charge clients. On the whole, the industry operates on a time and material basis, but I suggested that they could operate by licensing out their creative assets. So rather than clients paying for a creative's time to come up with the latest advertising idea, was there a model whereby the client licenses the creative output so that there is ongoing revenue for the creative idea?

I was met with, 'That's not how it is done.' Interestingly also in that organization, they had a very narrow idea of what data should be used for, as that is what the senior leadership believed data could only be used for. They had never considered data being used to support or spark creative ideas, or data being used to inform the strategy. Data was always used to evaluate what they had delivered, and that's how they had always done that.

Throughout the book, I will provide some guidance and strategies on how to change an organization so that a healthy data culture can be nurtured, from how the data team is positioned and promoted internally, to what processes to put in place so that organizations begin to adopt a data culture. But from my experience, even now, I still work with organizations where there is a committed ambition to use data and its latest applications but no willingness to change the organizational culture to accommodate a data culture.

Countering the HiPPO

Early in my career I was introduced to digital analytics. On that journey I came across the term HiPPO. It was used by many digital analysts to speak of someone in an organization, whose opinion would carry more weight than facts. HiPPO stood for highly paid person's opinion (or if used with an uppercase I, as in HIPPO, it stood for highly important person's personal opinion). I believe the former is the more common definition.

This brought home to me how much individuals impact company culture, how very senior individuals can make or break a data culture. With all the will in the world, a company with one or more HiPPOs can undermine the hard work that the data team and also the wider organization may be doing to become data-driven. I have been fortunate not to have come across many HiPPOs in my career, but I have heard tales from other data leaders and especially data analysts of how entire meetings would be hijacked by senior stakeholders who believed that their views and opinion were correct and that the data was just an inconvenience. Sometimes, even worse, the HiPPO may have been influenced by someone else and they then regurgitate that opinion without any regard for how factual it is.

In one example, it was relayed to me that a very senior person in an ecommerce business would periodically ask the marketing team to promote certain items they had for sale on the homepage. When asked why, the senior person said their wife had told them that it would be popular, and when asked how she knew, apparently all her friends were talking about it.

The data never showed that what they promoted resulted in more incremental sales, but the HiPPO never listened to the data, and therefore was not engaged in learning, and so would then voice opinion after opinion, expecting time, effort and resources to be allocated to their ideas, with no evidence that they worked, and frustratingly not wanting to learn.

The need to establish a data culture

A good data culture ensures that the opinions of certain highly influential individuals in organizations becomes a rarity, and if other senior leaders understand that they need to work with data to be successful this person may also begin to understand that. If data is presented consistently, and sometimes persistently, to help the business learn from its past, plan for the future and execute with confidence then it will be harder for individuals to operate outside the data culture without feeling like an outcast.

A data culture will reinforce the importance of being data-driven, of what it means to have an open mind about what is known now and what can be learnt through experimentation. It allows data analysts and leaders to be part of the decision-making process and not a back office service delivery team who only react to data demands. A healthy data culture fosters collaboration, as success and failure is transparent, and data is not seen as a weapon to be wielded to win points, but rather to demonstrate collective success.

Organizations often overlook this aspect of their data journey, and when making decisions on who to hire, what technology to buy and even what data to collect, they haven't thought through the values, beliefs, practices and behaviours that the organization will align on to leverage that data most effectively.

References

Binet, L and Field, P (2013) *The Long and the Short Of It: Balancing short and long-term marketing strategies*, Institute of Practitioners in Advertising, London

Kahneman, D (2011) *Thinking, Fast and Slow*, Farrar, Straus and Giroux, New York

Saxe, J G and Galdone, P (1963) *The Blind Men and the Elephant*, Whittlesey House, New York

Why analysts and technology are not enough

3

I have often seen companies fail at being data-driven because they did not create the right data culture. This was mainly a result of believing that being data-driven or utilizing data for decision-making starts with hiring lots of analysts and buying the latest technologies. It's a trap I see a lot of companies fall into. It's the same belief that leads to many digital transformation projects failing or taking longer than expected, or even, when they are delivered, the company not reaping the benefits.

However, when you begin your data journey, there is a temptation to just get on with it. Hire a data lead, or a senior analyst, build a team around them and then buy the necessary technologies to collect, store, process and present the data in valuable outputs that the business can use to make decisions or even to make automated decisions. Some companies even bypass the analyst part, buying technologies such as website personalization tools or marketing automation tools, which can target the right content to the right person at the right time.

However, over time they learn that these technologies do not deliver the value or return promised, because the organization is not set up to benefit from the insights and knowledge being generated from these systems. The main reason for this is that the organization has done what it believes it needs to in order to become data-driven, which is hire data people such as data analysts and data scientists, and they have been equipped with the tools to do the job. Beyond that, the rest of the organization doesn't believe it has a role to play in being data-driven, and that data-driven or better evidence-based decision-making will just happen automatically.

Julie Screech summed this up well when she said that organizations shouldn't be thinking of being data-driven as 'what we are' but 'who we are'. That is, it can't be a bit of an organization that is data-driven, rather it has to be part of the organization. So, some teams can't say they use data to make decisions if others say data has nothing to do with them. Julie's sentiment resonated with me – I've seen data teams and data activity siloed to certain parts of the business while other parts carried on as though the data team didn't exist.

The need to nurture data culture

During my interactions with different organizations where I have been asked to either build out a data function or develop a data strategy for a part of the business, I have found that most of my time has been spent with the business nurturing the data culture. I spend a lot of time with different people around the business explaining how the data they have can help them in various ways.

If you are a new data leader you may think that your main task is to get a team in place, and start analysing data to deliver value with the tools at your disposal. However, you will quickly learn that, without buy-in from other parts of the organization, your work and that of your team is sidelined or limited to specific use cases. This then hinders your ability to influence the business and make an impact.

For any data leader tasked with building out a data function in an organization to help the business deliver the vision of being data-driven or basing decisions on data, the first thing to establish is what proportion of the business is aligned with these strategic goals. This will go beyond just establishing that others can recite the strategic goals for data, or provide generic expressions of interest in how they want to use data. You need to establish that they have thought about the ways of working, how they will interact with the data team and access the data, what their KPIs are and how they expect them to change by utilizing data.

This requires not just meeting all the teams within the organization once and introducing yourself, but building long-term relationships in which the environment is conducive to them asking you and your team questions and you and your team being able to contribute to solutions to the challenges they have. The aim is not for you to be a problem solver, but someone who represents and can contribute to solutions from the data perspective of the organization. It is therefore essential that you set limits at an early stage about what your team will and will not do, as this ensures that different teams know how and when to engage with your team.

When you lead a data team or function you will find that over 50 per cent of your time is being an ambassador for data, internally and externally. To do your job effectively you need to have established some clear visions on what you hope to achieve. This goes beyond some use cases, which may be the building blocks for how you get started, to a grander vision of the use of data.

A vision for data

As a data leader, if you are not clear on what you hope to achieve then it will be difficult for the data team or your organization to truly understand what being data-driven hopes to achieve. When I set up the data team at ITV as Head of Business Information, I was given the tools needed to analyse data from the new ITV.com website and the ITV player, as well as budget to hire a couple of data analysts. Building a team was relatively straightforward, and settling on tools which did the job was a case of making a selection.

However, the constant challenge was getting the business to use data for decision-making. It wasn't and still isn't the case that you become a data-driven organization just because you have data. Over time I realized that the organization needed a vision about the use of data. It was essential that I was able to communicate the importance of data-driven decision-making, driving growth, efficiency, and customer satisfaction through the use of data. From this vision I was then able to translate into exemplar use cases, so that different parts of the business could see how data was important to them.

It also went beyond the users of data, though it did impact most parts of the organization. It also required being in constant communication with teams who were responsible for the collection and storage of the data, those that would have more impact upstream in the data chain. In ITV and other places, I set in place a vision for the use of data. These ranged from complicated, such as showing how data can be used to create and capitalize on commercial opportunities from content creation, delivery and optimization to more simpler vision statements where we talked about creativity infused with data.

It was never the case that we had to have a fully fledged vision statement which we had worked through with intricate details of what we wanted to do with data in every part of the business, but rather a broad enough statement that allowed the business to get behind was critical. It is also important that you understand the limitations of the vision for data, as in some, if not most, businesses you will find that what you think the potential for data may be is not what others in the business think.

In some businesses there will be teams or departments who openly state that they don't believe that data can help them do their job better. These are typically departments where ideas are the product, whether that be a TV show, an article, an advert or something that is a product of human creativity or ingenuity. In these cases, it is best not to preach but for them to just observe what you do in other parts of the business, and if they can see any value they will approach you. In my experience this has worked best, as when I have directly engaged with these teams, the initial resistance takes a disproportionate amount of time to counter, energy which would be best spent on other parts of the business.

In setting a vision, establish with senior leaders and your peers what the vision is for data in your organization:

- Is it to be better at decision-making?
- Is it to deliver a better customer experience?
- Is it to create products which automate processes?
- Is it to save time and money by being more efficient?
- Or is it to do something else?

Whatever you decide, ensure that it is feasible. I've worked with many organizations who have set lofty goals and ambitions for data, with an overarching vision, but haven't worked out how they will execute it. For example, a very large organization set the ambition that all decisions would be data-driven; with thousands of employees doing a variety of roles, they were not clear how this would translate into actual day-to-day ways of working. Though the vision to rally the organization behind a clear purpose for data was a good one, there was not wide consultation of how this would work.

It's a good idea to also converse with colleagues from different departments and roles to understand what they do, how they do it and the potential for using or leveraging data. It may be that you have an ambitious vision, but be very clear which teams it would start with, and then how it would be rolled out across the whole or-ganization.

Or you may decide that at a minimum the vision should be that where data is available everyone in the organization should use the data as part of the decision-making process, so something like 'mak-ing decisions with data'. Or you may decide that the best data you have is from your digital properties or transactional systems, and have a narrower vision such as 'using data to understand our cus-tomers'.

Whatever is decided, it should ideally be done with an understand-ing of how different parts of the organization are likely to translate the vision statement and then use the data. This needs to be commu-nicated regularly so that over time it becomes part of the organiza-tion's data culture.

Data literacy

For the organization to gain maximum value from utilizing data, in-dividuals in the organization need to have some data literacy, that is, understand what the data is telling them. There should be a will to invest in training that helps people to interpret data and draw mean-ingful insights. Now, when you suggest this you are more than likely to get a response along the lines of 'that data is for the data team and others do not need to learn about it'.

But data literacy is not about people being data analysts. It means that they understand the data. This requires non-data people and teams to gain a grasp of what different terms mean and how data is calculated. Take, for example, the metric of 'visitors' and 'unique visitors'; most parts of the business do not understand why they can't just add up daily visitors to get a weekly number. Too often, after delivering or presenting the results of some analysis, I have seen analysts having to explain what certain terms mean, how they are calculated and how they should be used. This turns what should be decision-making meetings into data lessons and derails the purpose of the insights being generated. In this instance, it needs to be explained that a visitor can visit on several days, and at a daily level will be counted in each day they appear, but when looking at the data across a week they would only be counted once and not counted multiple times because they visited on multiple days in that week.

One way to position improving data literacy in an organization is to also suggest that the data team are proficient in understanding finance, marketing, sales, product, technology, etc. In my opinion, data teams have no choice but to be literate in understanding how other parts of the business operate. Data cuts across many departments, and so data teams need to understand how those parts of the business operate. The same is also true the other way, that different teams need to have some basic data literacy.

Julie gave a nice example when discussing data literacy. She said that when she moved to a foreign country, she tried to learn the local language. She was open about experiencing the culture and learning the local language would aid her in that. She found that some of her peers who also relocated to this foreign country had not made any effort to learn the local language, and this was a broader indication that they were not also open to learning about the local culture. With data culture it is the same – if your organization claims that it wants to be data-driven or use data for decision-making or even data for efficiency and effectiveness, then the people in that organization need to learn the 'language' of data. This should be reflected in how people behave in the organization, from onboarding a new employee to engaging with outside partners and agencies. She reiterated that as an organization you become it, not just use it.

Create a glossary

A common barrier to data literacy is knowing where to start. It's not always feasible to send everyone on a training course to learn fundamental concepts of data, nor would it be practical, as the data in your organization and how you use it will have nuances that a general data literacy training programme could not capture. I've often found when working with organizations that some reports or dashboards are already being delivered, or that some teams are using data from systems that generate their own reports. The metrics and KPIs in those reports and dashboards serve as a good starting point for improving the data literacy of an organization.

Before I discuss how best to go about this, it is worth noting two major points. The first is that, for each organization, how they define metrics and KPIs in their glossary of data terms will be specific to that organization, and secondly that for many organizations, if not all, this should not be a static document, and therefore it should always be a live, work in progress, document that can be updated by a select group of people at the required intervals.

A glossary of data terms is a business-friendly way of describing what each metric means. It should contain how metrics are calculated and how they should be interpreted, with an example if required. If your organization already has reports or dashboards, then that is the best place to start to compile your glossary of data terms.

The exercise you should conduct is to create a table with four columns (Table 3.1):

- Column 1: The metric or KPI – just name it as it is stated in the report.
- Column 2: A short description of the metric or KPI – use plain English and avoid any technical terminology.
- Colum 3: If required, give an example of what the metric of KPI may look like – this is only required where the KPI could be a list or selection of variables (e.g. marketing channels, store names, etc.).
- Column 4: A list of what else this metric or KPI may be known by – within the organization it should only be known by the metric in column 1, but outside the organization it may have another name or in a third-party system it may be labelled under a different name.

Table 3.1   Example of a data glossary

Term	Description	Example	Also known as
Visitor	An individual visiting a website during a period of time		User, browser
Visit	The number of times a site is visited		Session, traffic
Page view	The instance of an internet user visiting a particular page on a site		Hit
Time spent	The amount of time, typically in minutes, spent on the website	03:00, 01:45	Minutes per visit
Bounce rate	The percentage of visitors who leave the site after viewing only one page	45%, 20%	Single page visit
Referral	The location the user was before clicking to the website	Home, External	Referring domain
Conversion	The point at which an activity or response to a call to action fulfils the desired outcome	Purchase, sign-up	Funnel
Keywords	The words that search engines associate with pages on your website		Search terms
Organic search	Describes searches leading to your website from free listings on search engines		Free search
Paid search	Describes searches leading to your website from paid listings on your website		PPC
Event	The recording of a particular action	Video play, click	Action

In my experience, this works well as it provides a starting point for your data glossary, and in the early days you can attach or link the glossary of data terms to the relevant reports or dashboards. You can then grow or amend the glossary as new metrics or KPIs are introduced and old ones may be retired. However, I would still keep any old data terms not being used as it can be a good reference point for any historical data discussions.

The alternative is to start from scratch and build your glossary of data terms based on all of the metrics or KPIs that the business is likely to use. You make a start with the most common ones and then over time add more to the glossary as they get used or discovered in old or infrequent reports.

What I have discovered is that if you aim for a company-wide consensus on these terms then it is unlikely you will ever find one, and, on a practical note, it can take forever. Therefore, my practice has been as a data leader to start the glossary and then consult my team to add, amend or refine what I have created. Once we as the data team are in agreement, then we present it to the business. However, I wouldn't recommend presenting all of it to every team. My suggestion would be to only present the relevant metrics and KPIs to the relevant teams. There is no point in getting the view of the product team on how finance calculates revenue, or how marketing calculates acquisition.

I am making this sound simple, and many of you will acknowledge that it can be a mammoth task, as not only will you encounter disagreement in what the data team has deemed the definition and the respective departments, but also disagreement within departments. My advice is to embrace it, as you can use it to show why you need to create a glossary of data terms, and that once we have it, even though it will take effort, that it will help the organization move forward.

The opposite can and may occur, which is that you get nothing or very little feedback from the different departments. In this instance, I have found that promoting the glossary when presenting or sending out reports and dashboards gains some traction in people looking at it and then commenting on either data terms they do not agree with or questioning data terms they do not recognize.

As mentioned previously, you cannot expect to create a final glossary of data terms; it has to be a work in progress. Therefore, it should be made very clear from the outset that what you are creating is something that will be regularly updated and reviewed by the data team as well as in consultation with the different teams. The other thing to also note is that for some teams the metric of KPI may not change, but how they are asked to calculate or create it may do. In these cases, I would recommend you maintain some version control to note when the definition, calculation or creation of the metric changed, so that old reports and new ones can be compared with an understanding that the same metric may mean a different thing now to what it did before.

So, how do you make this glossary of data terms a work in progress and a living document? Well, it's much easier now than it was before, with cloud-based document creators. You could use something as simple as Google Docs or Sheets, or Microsoft Office Word or Excel. You could create the glossary in the online version of these tools and share with the organization, either within reports and dashboards or separately when needed. You ensure that some are allowed to make changes, others to add comments and the majority would just be reviewers.

Who makes changes and who can add comments will need to be left to each organization and data leader to decide. My preference has been that only a handful of members of the data team should be able to make changes, with two or three individuals in each department allowed to comment. These comments will be reviewed, and if necessary questioned and interrogated by the representatives of the data team before the glossary is updated.

There is a temptation to accept all comments from the different teams, as the data team may believe it is their KPI and therefore they would know what it means. I wouldn't do that. It is always useful to ask a few simple questions:

- Where does that metric or KPI come from (is it an internal or external/partner system)?
- Has it been adjusted in any way (e.g. converted to a percentage, has the source system filtered any cases, is it calculated from other metrics, etc.)?
- Do we have access to the raw data that creates this metric?
- Where did you get the definition from?
- Has your whole team agreed upon this new metric or KPI definition?

If you find the commenter who wants to add this KPI or metric or change an existing one can provide satisfactory answers, then you can confidently make the changes. If they cannot then it is worth doing your own investigation as a data team into this new or changed metric definition to satisfy yourself.

As mentioned, try to keep version controls of metrics or KPIs that change so that the organization can refer back to previous definitions if needed.

For those organizations which have collaboration software such as Atlassian, then use tools within it such as Confluence to create a glossary template and then use that to maintain a live glossary. The benefits of these collaboration tools are that they have workflows built in, which allows you to assign tasks to people. This means that if you wanted to make a change to, say, a marketing KPI based on a comment, you could assign a task to someone senior in marketing to review your new definition and have them approve it, or not.

Single source of truth

One of the biggest challenges that arises with a glossary is when the business has two or more systems which measure the same thing. This usually occurs when third-party tools are used to collect the data and the business is not in control of what is being collected. A common example I encounter all the time is to do with visitors or users to a website. Most companies that have a website will have a digital analytics solution on their website, such as Google Analytics or Adobe Analytics. A core metric that these systems produce is a count of how many visitors or users came to the website.

They may calculate this differently and often will, but if you use one of these tools, then the calculation is consistent and you can confidently report on changes to visitors to your website over time. An issue can arise, because the sales team may also be tracking the website through an ad server which will also have a way of counting visitors, which is definitely going to differ from how the web analytics tool does it. The marketing team may also have their own marketing attribution solution tracking visitors, and the product team may have another solution for measuring customer experience which will also track visitors.

All these solutions will measure visitors differently and you could potentially have three or four measures of visitors to your website. That is why it is essential that you agree upon a single source of truth for each metric.

Where I have encountered these scenarios, I have worked with the organization to agree upon a single source of truth, but also allowed the other metrics reported by the systems used by the different teams to also be used, but we have compromised on naming them differently. So, typically, the digital analytics tools have always been the source of truth for visitors, and we usually agree that visitors numbers from other systems are not reported, but if they need to be then they are labelled differently. So, for example, if the sales teams wanted to use the visitor numbers from the ad server as it allows them to quickly make conversion calculations in the ad server to optimize ad delivery, then this metric would be labelled as something like 'ad server visitor' or 'ad server cookie', referencing how visitor number is created in the ad server.

I have also encountered scenarios where the same system can yield different numbers for the same metric. For example, working on a client's customer relationship management (CRM) system, I encountered two different numbers for 'total customers' in their reporting solution. Both were labelled as 'total customers' but the numbers for any given month differed between 15 and 20 per cent. Through enquiries, it transpired that the larger count of total customers came from a count of unique customer IDs in the CRM system, whereas the lower number came from a count of unique customer IDs after all internal employees, partners and test IDs were extracted. The reason was that this organization was a very large conglomerate and all employees and employees of partner organizations were automatically enrolled in the loyalty system to benefit from exclusive discounts within the suite of brands the conglomerate owned.

The two versions of reporting total customers arose because the business wanted to show growth in their loyalty programme, and so in the early days all employees and employees of partner organizations were automatically enrolled. The growth of the loyalty programme looked impressive. Later, when growth slowed, the loyalty team wanted to know the 'true' loyalty customer base and created the logic to exclude internal and partner employees, plus all test IDs. This immediately reduced the total customer number base, but the loyalty team were unable to monitor the actual growth in loyalty customers.

Now, it could be argued that either could be the true number – internal and partner employees were also customers of the brands the conglomerate owned, so they should be included, even if they are automatically enrolled. The other is also true, that as they are automatically enrolled they shouldn't be included as they aren't real loyalty customers.

In the end we decided that we needed to create a different definition for customers based on a new calculation. We still had total customers, which included internal and partner employees, and everyone agreed to omit test IDs, which were very small anyway, then a new metric of active customers was introduced reflecting customers, including internal and partners employees, who had transacted with the loyalty programme in the last 12 months.

Introducing the 'active customer' number allowed the business to get used to a smaller number of customers, but a more relevant number for operational purposes, as they could differentiate between those customers who signed up to the loyalty programme automatically or actively and continued to stay engaged, as opposed to those that did not. The 'total customer' number was and I believe still is used for public relations (PR) purposes to show how big the loyalty programme is, whereas this new metric of 'active customer' is used internally to understand the true health of the loyalty programme.

Caveats and limitations

A glossary would never be completed if caveats and limitations of the data were not included in the description of each metric. I wouldn't go overboard on this element, but for some metrics and KPIs it is useful to include any caveats and limitations. The reason I mention this is that sometimes what we call a metric of KPIs does not actually reflect how that metric is calculated. I go back to the visitor to your website metric. A visitor to a website was typically measured using cookies, but more recently Google Analytics has introduced some artificial intelligence which can also track a visitor if they block their cookie. But, nonetheless, a visitor is not really a visitor; it is a digital identifier and if the same person deletes their cookies, and uses a different browser or device, then they will be counted as multiple visitors, even though they are just one person.

The reason you may want to mention that a visitor is calculated in this way is that some businesses will be based on historical measures of visitors or audiences using panel methods. TV is an example. The BARB panel measures people, and so executives in broadcasting may assume that the audience numbers they get for TV viewing and the visitor number they get for website performance are measured in the same way.

However, as I have mentioned, this is not something I believe needs to be highlighted and brought to attention. If you have ensured that you have a single source of truth and that the organization use the correct data terms, then how those metrics are collected, created or calculated is not such a big deal and most of the senior leaders, in my experience, are not really interested in the detail so long as they can trust the data when making decisions.

But do include caveats and limitations where it can impact decision-making. Take the example of reporting margin or profitability. It is always worth adding any caveats or limitations of how this is calculated. Don't forget, it's unlikely as the data team you will be able to replicate the calculation for margin or profit of the finance team. That's because the finance team waits till the financial year end and then at a gross level uses total revenue minus total cost to calculate profit, and even then it will be before tax or after tax.

Establish key success metrics

A major part of having a vision about data is understanding what success looks like. Therefore, as an organization you should be able to demonstrate how the success of using data at each team and department level leads to success at the business level. An essential way to help the organization to understand why it's important to ensure that the accurate collection, storage and processing of data is maintained is through showing how each part of the business is responsible for the company's overall success.

If each part of the business understands the role they play in the business success through the KPIs they are responsible for then it motivates them to collect the right data, store and process it, and finally report on it to make the right informed decisions. During my career, I have had the good fortune to learn from a whole host of great people. One example was working with a couple of management consultants. I was explaining to them how I developed or was developing a data culture in the company I was working with at the time by aligning everyone's KPI to the overall business KPI, which in this example was profit. They then introduced me to the KPI pyramid (Figure 3.1), a method which provided a systematic process for the easy mapping of organizational KPIs to department and team KPIs.

Discovering this process was interesting for me as a learning experience. The practices you develop in your career are clearly influenced by the people you work with and the wider organizational culture. I had clearly picked up the principles of the KPI pyramid from people I have worked with previously. I must have been exposed to it at some point in my career, and even though I didn't know what it was, I knew how to use it in my own way. The same can be said for good data culture behaviours. Individuals may practise good data culture principles, through observation of others or working in an organization with a good data culture, without necessarily realizing that they are adopting the practices of a good data culture.

Anyway, the KPI pyramid is an effective method to visualize how the KPIs that different teams are measured on impact higher KPIs which then eventually impact the overall business's KPI. I always use this when designing reports or dashboards, but it is also a good way to get different teams to understand how the work they do will eventually impact the business KPI.

Whilst working at ITV, I had to use this KPI pyramid method to explain to a project manager that not tracking the performance of ITV Player (ITV's streaming service) on a platform they were about to launch would impact how KPIs were reported. It is often the case

Figure 3.1 A KPI pyramid

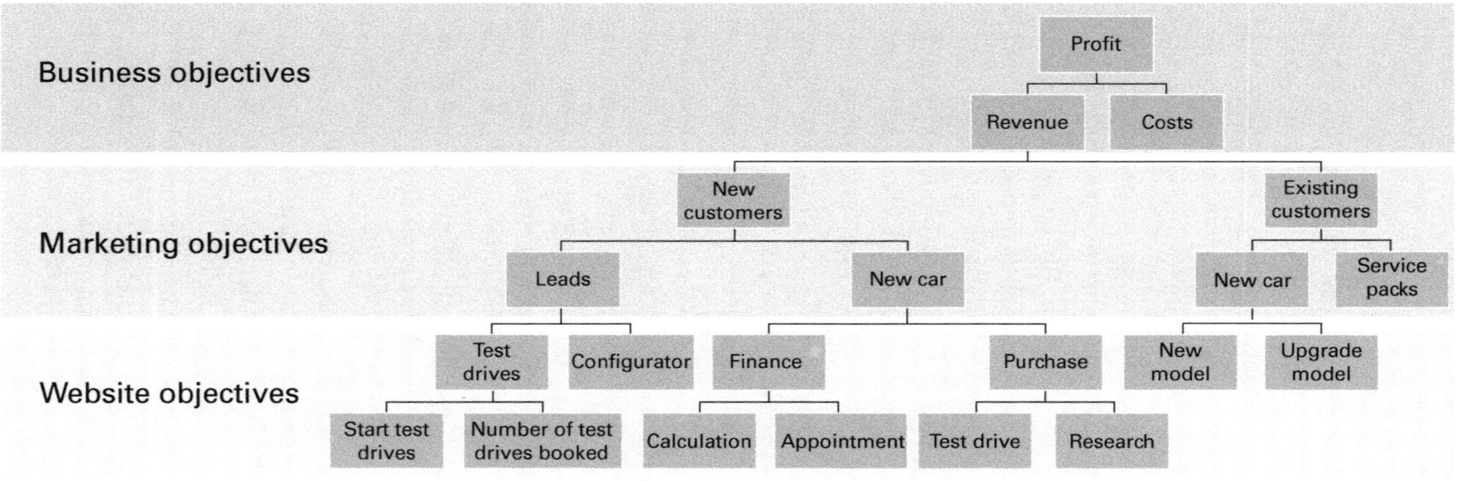

that collecting data is the last thing considered in a software development project, especially one that has myriad challenges. However, once these software products are launched, the first thing the business will ask is how it is performing. Therefore, using the KPI pyramid, I explained that by not tracking the ITV player on this specific platform (I believe it was the Xbox platform), the reports we delivered would not be accurate as they would be missing data from an entire platform, regardless of how low the viewing numbers were at the time assumed to be.

It was also explained that these reports went all the way up to the CEO, and the total viewer number we reported back to the business from ITV Player allowed them to determine a total reach number across the organization, and that it would not be complete with a platform missing, and in essence would be inaccurate.

Based on this information, the project manager ensured that tracking the activity from ITV Player on this platform was prioritized and that we could track activity from its launch. This was only possible because we had clear success metrics in place and were able to articulate how something measured in one part of the business impacted metrics at higher levels of the business. Measuring success metrics is also a good way for the business to determine whether the data it is collecting and, more importantly, reporting on is important and significant for the overall business objective. Often I hear that different teams want to measure and report on this metric or that metric, and by using the KPI pyramid you can evaluate the importance of measuring these metrics in relation to the overall KPIs of the entire company.

Whilst consulting for the CRM team of a bank, we were presented with a shopping list of metrics they wanted to measure from their customer data. What concerned me was not the metrics selected, as these seemed reasonable, but the volume. It seemed they wanted to report on everything they could possibly think about. I needed the CRM team to focus on some core metrics, which would allow them to report back to their leadership the success of the CRM programme, but the team were still able to report on what I termed secondary metrics for internal purposes to improve the effectiveness of the CRM

Figure 3.2   A simplified KPI pyramid in action

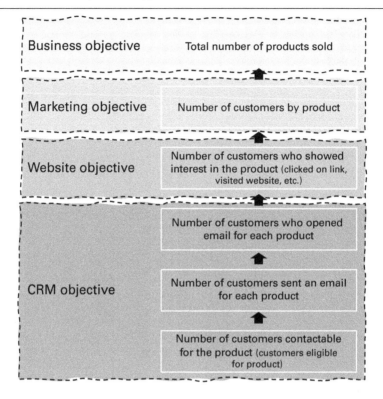

programme. These secondary metrics were probably not of interest to senior leadership, so we wouldn't include all of them in the reports that were presented upwards.

To do this, I did a simple exercise using the KPI pyramid. We knew that the business objective was to increase the total number of products sold to customers. This ranged from mortgages and personal loans to credit cards and savings accounts. Therefore, for the CRM team, the pyramid went something like the simplified version shown in Figure 3.2.

As can be seen, this helped the CRM team focus on what were the core metrics. Reporting on other metrics such as how many visits a customer made to a product, customers who showed interest in multiple products, customers who had not opened an email in the last three months, etc., were all interesting to know but were potentially secondary metrics and of use mainly for internal reporting and understanding within the CRM team to optimize the CRM programme.

Accessibility of data

One of the challenges that hinders the adoption of a positive data culture is access to the data itself. In my experience, frustration with the data team from other departments within the organization comes from the time it takes to deliver the analysis. In fast-moving businesses, where information is required quickly, if the data team cannot provide that information rapidly and in a timely manner then it is as though they cannot do their job properly.

Often this results in teams finding different ways to access the data, either through third parties, by bringing in specialist consultants or even finding other sources of data to inform their decision-making. Whenever I have encountered this situation, especially if my team or I have been brought in as a consultant to remedy this, I have had to establish whether the issue was with the team itself or with the systems and technology they used.

Occasionally, it is the team – they are either at full capacity and cannot meet the growing data demands of the business, but are unable to push back, and therefore seen as failing to deliver; or there have been instances where the team just doesn't have the knowledge or skills to get the data that is needed in time for the business to operate. In these instances, my team comes in and supports them, increasing capacity, but also then upskilling them so they become better at getting the data they need. In a recent example, we were working with a team who didn't have the expertise in using Google's BigQuery database, and so were struggling with getting certain digital analytics reports to the business as they were traditional digital analysts, used to using the interfaces available within Google Analytics, and so unfamiliar with Google's BigQuery. During the engagement, we helped them catch up on their backlog of reporting, fixed some reports that were broken and then upskilled the analysts to know how to extract the reports they needed from BigQuery.

However, the most common reason that data teams cannot provide data in a timely manner is that the systems do not allow them to do so. A poignant example that comes to mind is that I had a client who requested a report for the last 12 months for all of the 40 markets they operated in. The system we had access to was an on-premise Oracle database. They wanted the analysis within three days. The problem was that my team could easily write the SQL query to get the data the client wanted, but a single month for a single market took on average six hours to run. If you did the maths, that was $6 \times 12 \times 40$, so 120 days assuming we ran the queries 24/7. We looked at optimizing the query but the underlying infrastructure was just too slow to process the data fast enough.

Even communicating this to the client, they still believed it could be done. Unfortunately, it resulted in the client being disappointed as we were unable to deliver what they wanted. This failure was owing to the client not understanding that access to data was the problem, not the data team. Other instances I have experienced or witnessed is that the flow of data to the reporting systems is just not available in the timeframe the client or stakeholder expects it. In one such example, a daily refresh of a report happened at 10am for the day before. Therefore, at 4pm when the client wanted to know what had happened at 12pm that day, as they had launched a campaign that morning, the data was not available to explore performance of the campaign in the reporting tool. The client, however, was getting reports from the marketing agency, which had access to the marketing technology which delivered the campaign, so data was available within minutes. However, they did not track conversion on the website, which was done through an internal system that could only provide daily extracts at 10am the next day.

These situations make it difficult to win the trust and confidence of stakeholders, especially since they are not concerned with the details of how data flows between systems. It also makes it more difficult when some parts of the data ecosystem provide data more easily and in a timely manner than others.

Data access makes a huge difference to how the rest of the organization perceives the value of data and the data team and ultimately influences the data culture. Beyond standard data literacy of what data means, the data team should be involved in educating the business on how systems collect and process data. In several organization, such as Volkswagen Group and Henkel, I have delivered presentations explaining how data is collected by systems and how this data is then available for analysis. I then explain what they can do with the analysis, which is generally why they attend the presentation to begin with. By introducing these topics in a broader context of data analytics, you can start to socialize within the organization data platform and system challenges. Getting this right is not easy, but it helps if you can unify your data and provide consistent and seamless delivery of reports, so that data platform challenges are not something the rest of the business needs to worry about.

A data strategy

To get all of this in place and for most of this to come to life, as a data leader you will need to create a data strategy. I always advise my clients that, when creating a data strategy, they need to not only create one that works for the company, but one that also works for them and their data team if they have one. This is because the data strategy will be executed by them and their team and must reflect the values and beliefs they hold about data and what they believe is the full capability of data.

Delivering a data strategy, which creates a data culture which is not reflective of the people delivering it, can be hard. Therefore, it is advisable that the data strategy is created internally or at a minimum owned internally by the company, even if an outside consultant comes in to create it. I have created data strategies both as an internal data leader for companies, as well as a consultant. In both cases, I have always sought the views and opinions of the people who this will impact the most. That meant working with any internal data team, stakeholders from other departments, any partners who contribute with data and senior executives, who I always make sure at the outset are invested in being a data-driven organization.

If I did not do that it would mean that the data team, including the current or future data leader, will need to go against the data culture they have learnt and practised, and try to adopt one created by an external agency who did not take into consideration the people who this would impact. One of the things about a data strategy is that it provides a framework for how an organization can become data-driven and in that process how it develops its data culture. Therefore, a data strategy should reflect the company's ambitions about what it wants to do with data, with the strengths of the company, so that it focuses its data efforts where it makes the most impact.

Trying to achieve things with data where the company does not have a strength or where parts of the company cannot, or sometimes will not, use data, will result in a top-down enforcement of the use of data, which is never a good basis from which to develop a data culture. In this book I will not aim to detail what a comprehensive data strategy should encompass, rather I will provide a high-level view of what should be included in order to allow readers to begin the process of writing their own data strategy.

Building a data strategy

A data strategy refers to a comprehensive plan or framework that outlines how an organization collects, manages, analyses and utilizes data to achieve its goals and objectives. It encompasses various aspects related to data, including its collection, storage, governance, quality, integration, analysis and security. A well-defined data strategy helps organizations harness the power of data as a strategic asset and derive meaningful insights from it. It ensures that data is treated as a valuable resource and leveraged to drive decision-making, enhance operational efficiency, improve customer experiences, and gain a competitive edge.

Components of a data strategy may include:

- **Data governance:** This section should seek to establish the processes, policies and responsibilities for data management, ensuring data quality, privacy, security and compliance with regulations. An often-overlooked section, with responsibilities spread across several teams, the data leader needs to ensure that their organization takes this aspect of a data strategy seriously. An organization with good data governance practices, will also develop a healthy data culture, as importance will be given to the data itself, ensuring that clean data is collected, stored, maintained and used.

- **Data architecture:** In collaboration with the IT team, the data leader should set out their vision for data to flow from source systems to the business. Then working with solutions architects, the data leader should design the structure and organization of data systems, including databases, data warehouses, data lakes and data integration methods.

- **Data collection and acquisition:** This section should identify sources of data, both internal and external, and define mechanisms for collecting and acquiring relevant data in a structured and efficient manner. This section may also contain aspiring data sources that the business may want to collect but which are not currently available or accessible.

- **Data integration and management:** Developing methods to integrate data from various sources, ensuring data consistency, and enabling seamless access to data across the organization. Often, this section may shortlist technologies that may provide the data integration and data pipeline facilities.

- **Data analysis and insights:** For most data leaders, this part provides an opportunity to show the business the value that can be gained from data. They should define the approaches for analysing data, applying data mining, statistical analysis, machine learning, or other techniques to extract meaningful insights and drive decision-making.

- **Security and privacy:** Another often overlooked section in a data strategy, this sets the tone for how an organization values the entities from which they collect data, whether that be customers, employees, partners or suppliers. Respecting the data of these entities demonstrates the willingness of organizations to foster a positive data culture. All organizations should implement measures to protect data from unauthorized access, ensuring compliance with privacy regulations, both domestically and internationally where relevant, and establishing protocols for data sharing.

- **Data culture and skills:** A specific section should be devoted to explaining how efforts will be made to foster a data-driven culture within the organization, promoting data literacy, and developing the necessary skills and capabilities to effectively work with data, as mentioned earlier. This section should, where appropriate, name and specify individuals or functions who will be champions of data or serve as advocates for data initiatives.

- **Technology infrastructure:** It is always worth having a section where the organization has evaluated and selected appropriate tools, platforms, and technologies to support the data strategy, including data storage, processing, analytics and visualization. The data leader should ensure that they work closely with the IT team and adopt corporate standards in technologies, so that they do not create their own technology estate, which they find is then not supported by the organization's IT team.

- **Performance measurement:** Finally, as mentioned earlier in this chapter, be sure to define KPIs to assess the effectiveness of data-related initiatives, monitoring progress and continuously improving the data strategy. This allows data leaders to reinforce the value of data when reporting back to senior stakeholders.

A robust data strategy should always align with the overall business strategy and consider the specific objectives, challenges and opportunities of the organization. It serves as a road map for leveraging data as a strategic asset and facilitates data-driven decision-making at all levels of the organization.

Data leaders who bypass this step will find that they are constantly having to convince people of the benefits of using data. Each occasion will present new challenges as individuals revert back to how they have done things and will use numerous excuses for not using data, ranging from not being able to trust the data to data is not relevant for what they do.

A manifestation of the data strategy

But just having a data strategy is not enough. How the data team and especially the data leader manifests that strategy plays a pivotal role in how organizations adopt a data culture and the pace at which they do so. I've witnessed this walking into organizations where a data strategy had been created, but the data team did not change how they did things. This meant that the organization saw things as returning to business as usual, and the old issues around data quality, availability and timeliness returned, resulting in parts of the organization being selective in what data they used, if they decided to use the data at all.

The other extreme can also be the case. A client who I had previously worked with, a CFO, brought me into his new organization to help develop their nascent data team. He mentioned that other parts of the business were finding it difficult to work with the data team though the work of the analytics team was up to the standard he was expecting, but the new senior leadership team brought in to transform the business found engaging with the data team a challenge.

After speaking with the data team, especially the data lead, the rest of the organization and reading the data strategy co-created by a third-party consultancy, it was evident why there was friction, but it was hard to convince the CFO and the data leader that this was a problem. The crux of the data strategy was the democratization of data across the organization. The consultancy brought in to create the data strategy found that the wider adoption and use of data for decision-making was hindered by access to the data in the way that the business needed it. Several options existed in the data strategy, including expanding the team to provide bandwidth so that the data team could deal with the volume of requests being made, or upskilling key personnel in the various teams to access the data directly and also outsourcing part of the data team's remit. However, returning to the crux of the strategy of democratizing data, the consultancy recommended a self-serve model using low code/no code reporting solutions. This recommendation seemed to be the one that the data team and especially the data leader felt was the best. How they translated these requirements was to procure a reporting tool, in this instance Tableau, and a process was put in place so that each request that the business made would be translated into a Tableau dashboard or report that the relevant business could then use to get access to the data whenever they wanted. This allowed the data team to control how the data was viewed, as they felt that there were many nuances in the data and that other teams having direct access to the data would not account for these nuances and therefore incorrectly report on those numbers. Building a report or dashboard in Tableau allowed the data team to stay in control of the data.

The data leader said that when this solution was proposed, it was a sensible means to democratize the data. It also meant that the data team and the data leader stayed centre in this process, as all requests for reports would have to go through the leader's team. However, it became quite evident after a few weeks that this was not working. The reason I quickly elicited was that the manifestation of the data strategy by the data team, though based on the recommendations of the data strategy and coming from the right place, did not translate well in real life.

The problem being that not all data requests can be or needed to be built in a Tableau report or dashboard. This issue impacted the marketing and product team mainly, although they did find benefit in being able to run their own reports, as it allowed them to see on a daily, weekly, monthly or even quarterly level how marketing activity was performing on their digital properties. They could run the reports when they needed to see how much traffic was being generated by different marketing channels and how they were converting.

However, they equally had a need for bespoke reports, and often these reports would only be required once or for a short period of time. An example explained to me by one of the marketing managers responsible for partnerships was that they wanted to see whether a new partner was worth working with. All they needed was a report that showed referrals from this partner and their conversion. The first issue was that the data from this partner was not in the company's data warehouse, a Snowflake database – it was supplied as a CSV file each day; and secondly, the specific request required some transformations and filtering of the data to exclude particular referral data.

The data team, when they received this request, began developing a solution to ingest the data automatically from the third party into the Snowflake database, and then build out the report in Tableau. With all their other commitments, and the time it would take to create the data pipeline and Tableau report a time frame of just over three weeks was given. The partner campaign at this point had been running for over a week and the marketing team needed to know whether they had a business case to continue with the partner after the four-week pilot. That meant that the first reports they would receive would be after the pilot had finished and so they wouldn't have had any opportunities to tweak or experiment during the pilot phase to see the impact on conversion.

Even with getting the request prioritized, the data team couldn't accelerate getting the daily CSV files automatically loading into Snowflake and were exploring with the partner whether they could access their database using an API or connector. In the meantime, the partner suggested that the client's marketing team just send them their data and they would create the report at their end, connecting their data to the client's, transforming it and applying the filters. The analysts on the partner's side were able to do this within a couple of days and were able to update it with new daily data relatively easily, delivering the reports regularly in Microsoft Excel each day.

This resolved the marketing team's immediate problem of getting timely data, and unfortunately it showed that the partner was not suitable for them and even with experimenting throughout the pilot they could not increase or improve conversion. Once the pilot ended they terminated the relationship with the partner. However, the data team was still working on a solution and when they delivered the final Tableau report it was at least over a week after the partnership had concluded.

This was a rather extreme example explained to me by the marketing manager. Other examples included just wanting a simple number quickly, but the data team always insisted on building it into a report. That number was also only ever needed once and so they didn't see the need for having a report as they wouldn't be running it ever again.

Over time, the data team became more entrenched in manifesting the data strategy through the building of reports as they believed this truly democratized data for the organization and allowed the business to be self-serving. However, the organization began to feel like the reports and especially Tableau the tool was hindering their ability to gain access to the insights they needed when they needed them. Also, some senior executives in the business mentioned that they just did not have the time or inclination to run their own report and in previous roles just expected the data team to email them a number or summary of the analysis they wanted.

In these situations, where the data team manifests the data strategy in a way that doesn't work for the business, it can result in an unhealthy data culture. Not because there isn't trust in the data – in most cases there is – but the organization just feels that the data team is too myopic in how they deliver data and the outputs of data.

Therefore, how the data strategy is manifested in the organization is hugely dependent on the data team and the direction of the data leader.

Ways of working

In my discussion with Lara Izlan for this book, she made a point that one of the many catalysts for a wider transformation within a business is the use of data. For many organizations, where they are embarking on a transformation, primarily a digital one, they would also be engaging in using and leveraging data in earnest, potentially for the first time. Therefore, it provides an opportunity for the business to use this to instigate wider changes.

To do this effectively, the data team and those tasked with ensuring data plays a core role in their operations, from marketing and sales to product and strategy teams, must incorporate the use in their everyday activities. It can't be as some organizations I have witnessed do, which is as a bolt on, only used when directed or if at the end of the process someone mentions that they should look at the data and then it is added to the agenda as an afterthought.

A good data culture will see people throughout the organization referencing findings and using data in their everyday tasks. The best example I tell my team of them having a positive impact in the organization is if they see their reports or dashboards being printed and carried by senior executives in the organization when they go into meetings. It shows that data is part of their armoury in making decisions and sends a message to the rest of their team the importance of that.

Having worked in various organizations, I have seen that organizations that have a healthy data culture are ones that don't see data as a separate part of the business. Rather, they see it weaved throughout the organization's way of working, from using reports and dashboards in meetings to conducting tests to learn what works and doesn't work to asking questions collectively as a business that requires data for answers.

Where to start when developing a data culture

4

It is rare to find an organization that doesn't have some form of data culture. It may be nascent or not well formed, but it will be the product of the individuals' past and present who have impacted it. We bring with us our history and experience, and the lessons we have learnt elsewhere. Part of that is how we make decisions or how we learn new things or how we discover new knowledge.

Though not everyone takes an academic approach to finding out about things before deciding what to do next, people try to evaluate the evidence they have before making a decision. There are obviously biases in how individuals evaluate information. Effects such as the primacy/recency effect where information that is presented at the beginning (primacy) and end (recency) of a learning episode tends to be retained better than information presented in the middle (Sousa, 2011). But even with these biases in learning, people will often use data or things they have learnt or witnessed.

It would, then, be expected that these data beliefs, values, practices and behaviours would carry over to the organizations that these individuals work in. When I started my first few roles, I was bringing the data culture I had primarily developed during my time at university and though others may not have developed their data culture in a structured way, they would have generally developed one. However, even saying that, organizations have a mixture of people and there will be those who probably have not developed a data culture because throughout their career they have relied on their knowledge, experience and expertise to make decisions and, on the whole, they have probably been successful. This could be because the knowledge and experience they have built is based on the casual use of data, assimilating knowledge and making decisions on what they have observed, or it is likely that the decisions they have made are not evaluated for success, so they believe they have always been right in their decision-making, even without checking whether that decision was a success.

More often than not, even in organizations where there is a strategy to become data-driven, as a data leader you will encounter senior executives and even not-so-senior staff who believe that they do not need data to make decisions or that there is not any value in data for the job that they do.

Start at the top

In situations where you have been tasked to transform an organization to be data-driven, your first task is to establish whether you have senior level sponsorship. Not the type of support that is only written in documents, but the one that is practised by the organization and that must start and be visible at the top. To become data-driven or to leverage data for your business and to build a positive data culture, the top levels of the business need to be convinced about the value of being data-driven. They also must practise it.

What I have found in my experience is that it is not enough to just meet once or twice with senior leadership as part of your onboarding or fact-finding sessions when you first join the organization and have been tasked with transforming the organization to be data-driven. You need to create an environment where you have regular interactions with senior level stakeholders and leaders in the organization. The first port of call should be your own manager and ideally also the sponsor of the data transformation programme. A significant issue, when trying to deliver a data-driven organization, is identifying the senior sponsor of this initiative. If you can't identify this person or persons, especially when interviewing or considering taking the role, then it's highly likely that data is not represented at the board level. Therefore, it is vital that the key sponsor is identified and that they also champion the use of data within the organization.

If there is no senior sponsor for data, then in smaller companies or where the data leader has access to the chief executive officer (CEO), chief operating officer (COO), chief finance officer (CFO), chief marketing officer (CMO) or equivalent, and this access is frequent, they should then identify a champion for the work they are doing and make them the surrogate data sponsor. In either circumstance the objective is to ensure that those at the top know what work is being done with data, what work the data team is doing and how data has had an impact on the business. Though you should focus on the latter, it is worth keeping senior executives abreast of the progress and work being done by the data team, as this keeps data front of mind for them.

The CEO of one of my clients when I started my data consultancies always wanted updates on what work we were doing. It could appear from the outside that these requests could be to keep track of our progress, but working with him it became clear that he would use examples of work we were doing to present at his investor meetings. It wasn't the case that he only discussed those that showed success, but he also wanted to demonstrate to the investors that they were an innovative and forward-thinking leadership team who were using the latest applications of data science and AI to make their company competitive and profitable.

Leaders such as this need to demonstrate that they are keeping abreast of the latest technologies and practices in the business world, and data is one of those. We even had an instance of demonstrating a prototype of an AI application which could decide when to offer discounts and when not to. Though the project did not move beyond the prototype stage, as we had not rolled it out to the wider business, the CEO was satisfied he could state that they were using AI to his investors.

Keeping the senior team informed, involved and excited is key to ensuring that data is thought of and discussed regularly, and even though it may not take centre stage in each meeting, it should be a key component of how the business operates. This then sets the stage for the rest of the organization to witness that the value of data and what it can do for the company comes from the top. As Fayez Shriwardhankar mentioned to me, you need buy-in across the business, otherwise the data function becomes a back-office tech support, and the team is typecast as used on a needs basis rather than driving the agenda. Data is then not seen as a side project which a company must do to show it is being innovative, or a vanity project of someone senior, but part of the wider business strategy. This starts with buy-in from the top.

Get stakeholder support

It is, however, not enough to keep the senior team informed and excited about data for a data culture to evolve in an organization; it is a necessary condition that you get stakeholder support. In my discussion with several data leaders, I have found that even if they are at the board level, they need allies or peers in other departments who will champion their agenda. If they are not on the board, they have said that unless they report to someone who champions the data agenda at the board level, they find themselves isolated and operating as another silo in the organization.

Therefore, getting stakeholder support is critical. This support should extend beyond just the senior leadership – it needs to permeate throughout the organization. It's worth pointing out that it's very rare that everyone in the organization will support the data agenda, and even though you may get uniformity in voices echoing how valuable they think data is for the business, the varying level of support from different stakeholders is to be expected.

Often when people discuss getting stakeholder support they usually refer to either senior level stakeholders or heads of teams who use the data. But your stakeholder is anyone in the organization who will interact with you and your team or the data that you use, in any form. Take for example the technology team, with whom data teams and especially data leaders will often need to work closely. There are often disagreements between ways of working, but without support from the technology team the life of the data team could become difficult.

One of the things you will learn when you work in data is that there are so many applications, plug-ins, services and systems you need to either access or install, but you may be limited in what you can do by IT policies.

With the technology team on board, the discussion around applications or systems that the data team needs becomes more constructive, because the technology team can see why the data team needs that application or plug-in to be installed on their laptop so they can do their job properly. I've always stayed very close with the technology leads and heads, so that when the time comes to ask for something, the discussion becomes a continuation of our existing data discussion and not something random and out of the blue for them. Often you will find that they can't allow the installation of an open-source application because it's against company policy, but if you have the support of the technology heads they will champion your need and even if they can't succeed will work with you and your team to resolve the issue in another way.

In one company I worked for, we wanted to download an Adobe Excel plug-in that was not an approved application within the organization and so the IT helpdesk was unable to install it for my team. However, since I had built a relationship with the head of IT, I explained why my team needed to install this plug-in, how it affected the work we delivered and the value to the business. This resulted in the head of IT making an exception and the trust built over time with this person and their team even went as far as allowing some of my senior data analysts to have local administrative rights to install applications and plug-ins themselves.

Getting support from just users of your data such as marketing, sales, product, corporate, finance, etc., is also too narrow an approach. You also need to work with teams who are the sources of your data. One such team is the customer services team. Often you find that to understand customer complaints and queries better, the customer service teams need to code and categorize the query accurately and consistently. However, if you ever observe a customer services operation, you will find that there is a pressure to resolve the customer complaint and then move on to the next one, so that the next person is not waiting too long.

Once a customer service representative has finished with a customer, they need to categorize the outcome of the call. If it was successful, they then code it as resolved, if it wasn't resolved and needs more investigation, it will be left as open. However, some queries are resolved but the customer is not satisfied and wants a follow-up or the issue is not something the company can do anything about, but the customer still has the problem. Often, to deal with these outcomes an open text field is provided. The details entered into this field determine whether the business could understand if there were any recurring related issues which they could investigate and improve.

When analysing the data for these issues, if the customers service representatives don't understand why the data they enter is important for customer satisfaction, then they are unlikely to enter much detail, resorting to entering comments such as 'needs further investigation', 'customer complaint not fully resolved', 'not related to our product', etc. These comments don't help the business to understand whether there is an underlying recurring issue which needs investigating or if these unresolved complaints are related or unrelated. This makes the work for data analysts that much harder. For one project, my team worked with the customer services team by demonstrating how we analysed the data they entered into these open text fields and how we could only extract insights the business could take action on if the quality of the data entered was detailed and accurate for analysis. These practical demonstrations highlighted to the customer services team the need for entering quality data and why what they entered mattered to the business, to successful KPIs, and helped them to understand what the business was therefore doing with that data.

Understand the business

This then brings us on to something that all data leaders and the data team need to develop, and that is their understanding of the business. I am still amazed when I speak to many data analysts, scientists and engineers about how their company makes money, especially ones where the product itself may not generate revenue directly. For example, in broadcasting and publishing, the content, whether that be a video or an article, is not the actual generator of revenue, but the adverts that are placed in or near them. I've experienced examples where data analysts have analysed data from ad-funded broadcasters' video on demand platform and claimed that fewer or no ads, or no ads before the content (pre-roll), would make the user experience much better. Undoubtedly this is true, but it would not make the company any money or it would reduce its capability to make money.

If the data team is not aware of how the business makes money or how different parts of the business operate, then the impact they are likely to have will be minimal. Worse, if the recommendations they make are not aligned with the business strategy they will be ignored. Understanding the business is crucial for a data team and this helps them become better and more effective data analysts.

There are many reasons why understanding the business is essential for all data teams:

- **Business context:** If you know why you are analysing the data then it makes it much easier for you to perform more meaningful and relevant analysis. You can also understand the specific goal and challenges of the business and tailor your analysis to generate insights that are more applicable and will lead to direct actions. Also, without a grasp of the business context, data teams may misinterpret the results. They might draw conclusions that are technically accurate but don't make sense from a business standpoint.

- **Relevant data:** When a data analyst understands the business well they can then easily identify what relevant data sources, KPIs and calculated metrics they need to answer the business question. By knowing the business's unique needs and constraints, data teams can design customized analytical solutions that cater to the specific requirements of the business. They can then focus on the data that matters, and deliver analysis and insights that drive business decisions.

- **Formulating questions:** Being familiar with how the business operates allows data analysts to formulate hypotheses for analysis. They can formulate questions that address specific business challenges and opportunities, especially when the business has difficulty articulating what they want in the form of a data brief. This hypothesis generation allows all the data analysts and the business stakeholder to have a common understanding of what analysis is being done, why, and what it will hopefully answer.

- **Strategic alignment:** A strong understanding of the business enables data teams to align their efforts with the broader strategic goals of the organization. This ensures that data analysis efforts contribute directly to the company's success. It also means that when the analysis is more aligned to the strategic goals then it is easier for the data teams to communicate their findings more effectively to their non-technical stakeholders, as they will be reflecting the strategic objectives in their findings. They can translate complex technical concepts into business terms, making it easier for decision-makers to understand the implications of the data for the overall business strategy.

- **Identification of opportunities:** An understanding of the business enables data teams to proactively identify new opportunities for data-driven initiatives that can enhance efficiency, customer satisfaction, revenue generation, cost savings and more. This is because analysis of the data can unearth potential insights that lead to novel or innovative thinking and allows new opportunities to be discovered. As data teams interact with the business, they gain valuable insights into what works and this understanding helps them refine their approach over time for better results.

An example of how not understanding the business or asking the right questions can lead to disappointment and stakeholders not being impressed, was relayed to me by Min Bhogaita, ex Director of Analytics at Deloitte, in our discussion. When he set up the Analytics Lab at Deloitte, they were new and not many in the business had heard of them. They did some promotional flyers asking people internally to come and check out the analytics lab. After three days someone came and gave them a CD of their data, and asked for some insights from the data.

Min and his new team were very excited to have got a request, and they started crunching the data and doing some analysis. When the internal stakeholder returned to see the results, they were not impressed with the output. The problem was that Min and his team didn't ask the stakeholder what question they wanted answered. In their excitement to get started with the analysis, they just analysed the data assuming what the stakeholder wanted, and their assumption turned out to be incorrect.

Min advises never to just analyse data without asking questions on what business objective the stakeholder or client wants answered. Even asking questions on how the business would use the information to make decisions or take action can lead to more meaningful analysis and insights. This also highlights that, when you have an evolving or weak data culture, you need to be aware that processes and practices will not be in place for the data team to question their stakeholders and understand what the business is trying to achieve. Later in this book I discuss how a good data culture provides the conditions for the data analyst to ask questions and understand what the business is trying to achieve, and then analyse the data accordingly.

Build trust

As you work with the senior leadership in your organization, collaborate with stakeholders and encourage your data team to learn more about the business. What you hope this achieves is trust in you, your team and the data. One of your objectives is to ensure that the analysis that you conduct and the findings that you present are trusted by the organization. Often in discussions with Stephen Kinsella we talk about how, when mentoring our data teams, we emphasize the need to ensure that they have confidence in the work that they do and the outputs that they produce. A common scenario many data analysts will encounter is when someone challenges their numbers or findings. People are entitled to question the interpretations of the findings, but as a data analyst you should always stick by the numbers you produce. If you show any lack of confidence in the numbers you produce, then you will lose the trust of people in the room and then it's hard for them to trust any further analysis you do.

Stephen even uses this scenario when interviewing prospective data analysts. He asks them what they would do in these situations. If they reply that they would tell the person they will look into the numbers and re-run the analysis, then people will lose trust in their work. If you are happy to present numbers, then you should be confident in how you got those numbers. If you are not then you shouldn't be presenting them in the first place. As I said, it's fine for someone to have a different interpretation of the numbers but they can't believe in a different set of numbers. That is just setting the company up to have a poor data culture, where individuals and teams can pick and choose what data they want to use and discard datasets that do not suit their needs. The correct thing to do is emphasize that the numbers are correct, you are confident in your analysis and therefore there is nothing wrong with the actual numbers. If the person doesn't agree with the interpretations of the numbers then they are entitled to have their own interpretation, as long as the numbers support that interpretation. What they can't do is have an interpretation that has no basis in the numbers, or believe that another version of the numbers would better suit their interpretation.

I have often encountered scenarios where sales, volume or customer numbers are going down. We have done the analysis and even though the data blips up and down month on month, over a long timeframe we can demonstrate from the numbers that there is a downward trend. We then get challenged by different teams that we are wrong and that sales are up, if they compare quarter on quarter or year on year. That is correct, but our analysis is over a longer time frame and shows a structural downward decline. So, even though their interpretation is correct if you take a shorter window of time, over the longer period which we have been asked to look at, the trend is downward. Therefore, anyone arguing against that will find that the only way to argue that the trend is not going downward is to argue that the data is wrong. We must categorically stand by our data and never allow anyone to question the validity and accuracy of the data. This doesn't mean that the analysis you do as a data team will always be accurate each and every time. Ideally you shouldn't make mistakes, and where mistakes are made the data team should own up and rectify, demonstrating that the mistakes are not systemic.

As I have always told my analysts, there can only be one right number and a billion wrong ones when doing any analysis, so make sure your analysis is accurate. If you end up making too many mistakes or you make mistakes at the wrong time, then you will lose the faith and trust of the organization, and therefore good data initiatives could fail because of this. I once had an analyst who worked for me at an agency. He was really good at what he did, but on a couple of occasions he made significant mistakes in his analysis. Unfortunately for him, those mistakes were made on the only occasions when he presented to the client. Owing to this, the client lost trust in his work and eventually we had to remove him from the account as too many questions were being raised about his ability to produce the right numbers, all because when he made a couple of mistakes they were in the presence of the senior stakeholder at the client side.

Trust is something that is a given when you are a data analyst – people expect you to be able to analyse data accurately. When you make mistakes, this can shatter people's faith in you to be able to do your job. Therefore, to gain the trust of your stakeholders and peers consider the following:

- **Attention to detail:** As a data leader you need to ensure that your data analysts pay attention to details. If they just skim over results or don't pay attention to their calculations, then they are likely to let mistakes slip through. So, being good at the details ensures that their work does not contain mistakes. This needs to be emphasized by you as the data leader to your team.

- **Listen to feedback:** Often your data analyst will be given feedback which may not seem relevant, such as providing the final number and not the working out, or presenting the data in a graph or chart that makes it easier to understand, or reducing the number of slides they are going to present. At the time, they may believe that the way they present their findings is the best way to do it, but often others can give insights into how best to present data in your organization. Therefore, it is essential that you explain to your data analysts to listen for feedback, direct and indirect, which can help them position their work in the best light possible and deliver it in the best format, gaining the trust of your organization that the data team know what they're doing, but also know how to do it in the right way.

- **Regular check-ins:** It is tempting for your data analyst to hide away whilst doing a piece of analysis to answer a significant business problem. However, this can have an adverse effect on others trusting their analysis, as people become uncertain about what they are doing. You as a data leader need to explain that the best course of action is to build in regular check-ins with their stakeholders, even peers and the data team, to discuss what they are doing, how they are doing it and what they hope to find. This then allows for feedback but also enables them to understand whether they are on the right track.

- **Be collaborative:** By working with different people across departments, your data analysts will be seen as a team who work across siloed departments and deliver results that apply across the business. This presence and behaviour will result in people seeing data as an enabler of the business and something that they should be involved with, fostering more trust in the data and in the data team. This collaboration should be a long-term thing and not just based on need, such as when a project needs to be delivered or some information sought. It should become a natural part of how the data team operates, rather than a separate initiative.

- **Transparent communication:** Successes and failures of data initiatives should be communicated on a regular basis. In Chapter 6 I discuss the need for a regular cadence of presenting analysis, from weekly, monthly and quarterly. This ensures that the organization is aware of what you are doing, learns from the failures and adopts the successes. It also ensures that the data team is visible, and is credited with the success of the business.

- **Learning loop:** This is something I encourage data leaders and data analysts to have in place wherever they work. As things evolve, and as the analysis that the data team does results in decisions being made, those decisions ultimately change the landscape and so therefore further analysis will reveal new insights or not support previous findings. Therefore, it is essential that data teams encourage a learning culture, where findings from analysis are communicated based on what has changed since the last analysis, feeding in any decisions that were made which are likely to impact the new analysis.

A predictive model I built for a client was based on understanding how many people who had joined through a promotion could be upsold a subscription. The model was then used to target and convert those customers to a higher tier subscription. Later, when the model was refreshed it failed to be predictive, because the people who the model predicted could be upsold a subscription were targeted by the CRM team and then subsequently converted to a higher subscription tier. Those that were left had a low propensity to subscribe to a higher tier, so when the model was refreshed it failed to be predictive. The marketing team had to be taught about how the model would need to be rebuilt as the current model was no longer applicable as they had changed customer behaviour through their targeted communications, based on what the previous model had prescribed. Don't forget, if you change your customers' behaviours, then don't expect historical behaviours to predict future behaviours.

Executional road map

Part of building trust in the data team and the data is being able to show results. Often, data strategies can seem theoretical, with possibilities included which are for the future and not now. When I asked several data leaders how they would execute their data strategy, they all mentioned that starting small and showing quick wins was far more effective than trying something big and transformational with data. In my experience this has also been true, but it does require a bigger plan to be also in play otherwise you end up with just lots of tactical projects and nothing that builds towards a larger data strategy. The best way to achieve those smaller and quicker gains is to build an executional road map (Figure 4.1).

Figure 4.1 Example of an executional road map

	Month 1	Month 2	Month 3	Month 4	Month 5	Month 6	Month 7
Quick win 1: Build manual MS Excel dashboards	◆						
Quick win 2: Build a one-off churn model			◆				
Project 1: Build data pipelines			████	████	████	████	████
Quick win 3: Automate MS Excel dashboards				◆			
Quick win 4: Automate churn model					◆		
Project 2: Build reporting platform		████	████	████	████	████	████
Quick win 5: Deliver Tableau reports							◆

An executional road map sits alongside the project plan, which shows how the data strategy will be executed but also shows the small projects that can be done before greater investment in people, technology or data is needed. Working with a broadcaster in the Middle East, I developed an executional road map that helped them realize the value of data from the video on demand (VoD) service. By analysing the data collected through their digital analytics solutions, we could produce insights which helped them deliver a better service without any further investment in technology or people. This provided the business with tangible outcomes they could see the benefits of, before moving on to the next one. These executional projects occurred alongside the larger project of centralizing the data from different systems, building a data lake and rolling out a reporting tool.

To build an executional road map, what you essentially do is look at the range of initiatives documented in the data strategy and also wider business strategy and start to isolate initiatives that can be done with the existing data, existing systems and tools, or with easy to procure and deploy tools and existing or freelance resources. The objective of an executional road map is to show some quick wins. Just like the executional road map developed for the Middle East broadcaster, we were able to quickly move from initiative to initiative based on the data they had and the systems they already had in place. As a data agency, we brought in new tools to the organizations, but these were tools that they themselves could have easily deployed such as Python, R and Tableau.

What differentiates an executional road map from a traditional project plan is that each initiative is just a separate small project, there is very little dependency between each project, and each project in itself demonstrates value to the organization.

Start small

Often with data projects, there is a temptation to do something innovative, such as using machine learning to personalize customer experience or provide recommendations in emails. However, these typically require some effort to acquire the data and also their execution can often be complicated. Therefore, to demonstrate immediate value, start small with projects that emphasize data-driven decision-making or where the outputs can easily be fed into technology platforms without much development work. These projects can demonstrate the value of data and act as success stories to inspire others. Typically, these pieces of analysis result in information and knowledge that allows the business to make decisions that result in moving towards achieving a business goal, but can also be precursors to more advanced projects in the road map.

A good place to start small is to create a list of the questions that the business wants answers to and start to answer them. This may seem tactical, but what it does allow is for quick results. In my work with large organizations with multiple stakeholders, interest can wane very quickly. So it is essential that results are delivered fast. Obviously don't sacrifice quality, but if you were to list out the questions the business wants answers to, you will find that many of them are not that difficult. I have encountered situations where the business would just like to know how many unique customers it has across its portfolio of products and services. This business knew how many customers each product and service had, but many of its customers held multiple products, but because data was held in different systems, no one was able to answer this simple question. It took an analyst less than a week to extract the customer data from each of the products and services and create a de-duplicated list of customers, telling the client not only how many unique customers the business had across all of its products and services, but also how many of those customers held a single product or service and how many held two or more.

This starts to answer very simple business questions which demonstrate to the business the value of data and of the data analyst. Though you can do many things quickly and make a big impact, there will be instances where the business question requires more time and effort. In this instance, my strategy is to create a project plan and present to the business the time and effort required to answer this business question, highlighting when I will have updates to share with them. At this stage, the business may decide that they want to put their efforts elsewhere or that they are happy with the time and effort required to do this, so will be content to wait that bit longer.

Reporting

An often-overlooked aspect of building a data culture is the cadence of reporting provided to the business. No matter what company I have worked in or with, there has always been an element of reporting and many of these reports are delivered at a scheduled time. In Chapter 7 I will explore in more detail how creating a cadence of reporting can create organizational change, but here I will discuss briefly how delivering reports is an excellent way of showing the business the value of data and of having a data team, which can be easily delivered.

My work across organizations large and small has taught me that if you can deliver regular reports, the business can immediately appreciate why it needs a data team. These reports serve as a visual reminder to the people across the organization of the work that the data team delivers. Even if the reports are automated, the business understands that there is a team that ensures that reports are sent out regularly. Another aspect of sending out reports regularly is that it starts to get the business used to seeing business KPIs. This exposure eventually changes the company's data culture, whereby if unsubstantiated statements or views are expressed about how the business is performing or what is working or not working, the availability and accessibility of data through reports makes challenging these unsubstantiated statements and views easier.

It even allows senior leaders to be challenged as often reports can be directly referenced as supporting evidence, without making it a case of individuals disagreeing. Where companies do not have a strong cadence of regular reporting, I often find that the data culture is weak and that, subsequent to a statement or view that is made which seems weak, analysis is conducted after the event to challenge this statement, and by then the time elapsed has meant that decisions have already been made or people have moved on.

Reports, however descriptive, play an important role in developing a strong data culture. When starting out, delivering reports, even if they are manually produced in Microsoft Excel, can have a significant impact in the minds of people moving toward a culture that uses and values data.

Focus on a single use case

As part of creating an executional road map, several use cases will be identified and prioritized. It is tempting to work on several at a time, and if resources permit there is nothing wrong with that. However, if an organization is only starting its journey in being data-driven, then typically their hiring plan will be to hire one or two data analysts. This then limits how much can be done, and so in this instance it would be advisable to start with one use case from the road map before moving on to the next.

If you can start with a single use case, as recounted to me by Abs Owdud, Analytics Director at Digitas UK, of his experience of developing a data team and culture at Quidco, then you find that later you can influence your stakeholders. In his case, he was brought into Quidco to do a customer segmentation, and even though when he spoke with the stakeholders they mentioned other priorities, such as what do our most profitable customers do, he created a backlog of requests and told the business that he would work on those after completing the customer segmentation.

Once he had completed the customer segmentation and demonstrated the value to the business of using data to create personalized emails based on the customer segmentation, he went about building a business case to address the other requests the business had, and based on the success of the customer segmentation and his business case he was able to hire another analyst. He found that starting small and focusing on a single use case, and making a success of it, allowed him to have influence with stakeholders to build out the data team.

Building an executional road map requires some flexibility in how you execute each of the business use cases or requests. It also may mean that somewhere during executing projects other priorities come to light that will need the projects in the road map to shift. It also will require the data leader to balance the available resources with the demands of the business and drive through a middle ground which keeps the business happy and does not stretch the team to the point where there is burnout or they decide to leave.

One of the challenges with working with data is that sometimes the answer to a very big business question can be just one number. To get to that number, however, could take weeks of work, work which is mostly invisible to the business. Therefore, having the opportunity to present a plan in the form of an executional road map to the business, with its updates and changes, helps the business appreciate the effort and work the data team is engaged in.

Data storytelling

Once you have stakeholder support, you need to keep them informed. It's all too easy to assume that once you get your stakeholders interested and supportive of your data endeavours, this support will always be there. In Chapter 5 I discuss how this is not always the case and that you can all too easily lose support. When you are speaking to your stakeholders and especially your senior leadership, don't assume that they will all understand the technical aspects of data analytics. There will be some who are fluent in data, with their literacy levels sufficient to understand, interpret and decipher the more technical aspects of data analytics, but assume that you are speaking with people who don't know the difference between weighted and unweighted means. Therefore, it is essential that you and your team don't rely too much on technical language and jargon to get your point across. It also helps if you can use the language of the business, so understand what is common in your business when referring to specific metrics and reflect that in the analysis that you present.

Part of storytelling is to understand what people are interested in. Any good story connects with the listener, and allows them to imagine themselves as part of the narrative. Min always encourages data analysts to do their preparation and understand what people are interested in. Therefore, as an analyst, being connected with the business and understanding the business is critical in order to be able to tell a compelling story about your analytics. I've sat in presentations where even though the presentation was not too technical it did not connect with the business users. I have also been guilty of doing this if I focus too much on what the analysis has accomplished rather than just simply answering the business question.

A few years ago, my team was building a behavioural segmentation for a client, hoping to understand how different users used their products. We were excited to discover some unique customer segments who behaved in a certain way that suggested that, if we could get them to visit one more time, we could convert a significant proportion to buy one more product. The team became so wrapped up in what the analysis showed and what was possible that we lost sight of what the business should do with that information. At the end of the presentation, the CMO asked what three things should they do with the information we had just told them. With so many recommendations in the presentation, we hadn't thought about what story we wanted to tell. We had told them lots of things, and arguably many of them very useful, but from the client's perspective it was just a list of findings and recommendations and not a cohesive narrative that would help them understand what was being presented, why and how they could use it.

Therefore, data teams need to be encouraged to develop the skill of storytelling rather than presenting findings in graphs and charts. The advice that Min gives is that you should do your preparation work and understand what people are interested in and then get to the 'so what' quickly in your presentation. Also, note that most leaders at large companies will claim that they are not technologists, so the language used in your stories must be relatable for them. The reality of storytelling is that you also have to learn to present slides of data, tables, graphs and charts as aids and not as the thing that you represent. Therefore, if you happen to have a table of numbers or a graph showing the movement of a metric, do not merely describe the data, rather provide a narrative that explains what the table or graph is telling you and avoid reading out the description of the table or graph. The best presenters of information are those that speak about the slides and do not read from the slides. This is something that data analysts are uncomfortable with, as they need the security of reading the actual content of slides to ensure that they have got all the numbers and results correct. But the art of storytelling is about getting across a message, an idea or viewpoint in a narrative that allows the listener to understand what you have done, why you have done it, what you found and what it means for the listener. The last bit is key – the story has to resonate with the listener. If they can't see the relevance of the story to them, then they will walk away without the data having any impact on what decision they make next. Note that if you do a good job in telling a story the audience will often just trust your numbers without feeling the need to investigate or interrogate them.

Assess data maturity

Whenever we work with clients to help them become data-driven in some form, we ask them to complete a data maturity questionnaire (Table 4.1). Data maturity is understanding from a people, process, practices and technology perspective where the organization is on the journey to be data-driven. Our objective in asking our clients to do this is that, by understanding the data maturity of the organization, we can tailor our solutions. The survey consists of three main areas relating to strategy, customer and capability. These are divided into sections and sub-sections, grouped to assess different aspects of data maturity. At the end of each sub-section, participants can add any further comments and thoughts to provide additional context to their answers. There are around 100 questions and typically it takes a participant no more than an hour to complete. The questionnaire should be completed by a broad range of stakeholders from across the client's organization.

The data maturity assessment evaluates the organization's maturity in terms of data capability and utilization. As the questionnaire is sent to individuals across the business, depending on response rates, it can also determine how varying levels of data maturity are perceived across the business. In many companies we run this assessment with, we have found extreme examples where some parts of the business believe that they are 'innovative' on certain aspects of the data maturity assessment, whereas others have stated that they are

Table 4.1 Example of a data maturity assessment questionnaire

Topic	Section	Sample sub-section	Sample question/statement per sub-section
Strategy	Direction	Vision	The organization has well-defined data-driven objectives aligned to the vision
		Strategies	The business has well-defined data strategies in place to meet its objectives
	Proposition	Brand	The brand and brand assets have been well and consistently executed in all channels
		Value propositions	The proposition fully utilizes data to improve the value and performance of delivery
	Insight	KPIs	The business has clear KPIs to measure customer experience
		Data integration	It is easy to connect the right people with the right data to support their decision-making
Capability	Marketing technology	Core systems	Core systems are being upgraded to support new digital demands
		Digital stacks and APIs	Digital services support the collection of all user data
	Technology	Platform architecture	To what extent does the organization leverage the full capabilities of the platforms it uses?
		Master data management	Does the business collect and manage its data in a consistent way?
	Operations	Optimization and innovation	There is a structured programme of technical optimization
		Skills	The business understands the skills needed to deliver its data initiatives

(continued)

Table 4.1 (Continued)

Topic	Section	Sample sub-section	Sample question/statement per sub-section
Customer	Lead generation	Programme and conversion optimization	The business can prove the value and contribution of all digital marketing channels
		Visible and owned media	Content is constantly pushed out to owned channels in an effective and automated way
	Experience and conversion	Omnichannel	The digital experience remains consistent no matter what channel you operate in
		Usability	Usability changes are underpinned by A/B testing (testing one idea vs another within a limited group)
	Engagement	Segmentation	The business has a segmentation programme for grouping like-minded audiences and customers
		Campaigns	The business has active campaigns which are executed across multiple channels

'basic'. This actually provides a good discussion point in understanding the data culture, and why such varying opinions exist.

The results of the data maturity assessment are provided in a table that allows an organization to see how it sits across the sections and subsections (see Table 4.2), and where data samples permit we can drill down into different departments and teams. The basis of the data maturity assessment is to allow organizations to have a view on where it is on the data maturity scale.

We have often found that the data culture in an organization is related to how different parts of the business rate themselves on their data maturity. In one example, we found that business stakeholders such as the sales, marketing and finance teams rated themselves low on the data maturity assessment, whereas the data and technology teams scored themselves relatively high. Through accompanying

Table 4.2 Data maturity assessment output

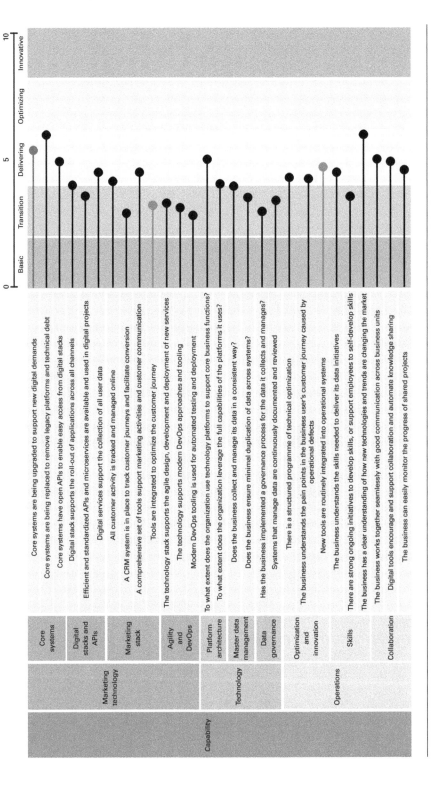

interviews, we explored the scores of different stakeholders in teams or individually, and discovered that the data and technology team scored themselves highly because they delivered answers, and specifically the data team, who said that they would always respond to requests with an answer.

However, in interviews with the various business teams, specifically the sales team, it was clear that the answers that were delivered by the data and tech team were not the answers the business was expecting. An example given was that the sales team needed to understand their audiences through a specific segmentation, which required using data from a third party. The data team, however, decided that they could recreate this segmentation or variant with just internal data, and that is what they did. When this was delivered to the sales team, it was not what the sales team had requested, but the data team was adamant that it would answer their question.

The data team therefore believed they had provided an innovative solution to something the sales team wanted, irrespective of the requirements and needs of the sales team, whereas for the sales team it didn't matter how innovative the customer segmentation solution, it was not what they had requested and definitely not something that answered the question they had, as the third-party data contained specific variables which they needed for a proposal.

On the one hand you had the data team believing they had delivered something that was innovative, whereas the actual business question was not answered. This example is symptomatic of a poor data culture, as there is no common understanding of why and how data is to be used, how the data team works with the rest of the business and the different perceived data maturity of the business.

As an organization, if you are keen to start a data-driven journey and transform your organizational culture to have a strong data culture, you do need to benchmark where you are now. The data maturity assessment we have developed at Be Data is one way of doing that. It provides for a check on the baseline of data maturity for different parts of the business and then a strategy for how to align the business and move everyone forward in adopting a positive data culture.

Build a network

Often when you are championing a data culture within an organization, especially one where that culture is just sprouting, it helps to know that you are not alone in that journey. It helps if you can find individuals within your organization who have potentially tried some form of transformational change that required developing a different culture, whether it is a data culture or otherwise. But that is rare to find, as typically data leaders are employed to start the journey and often you will need to look outside your organization to find people who have either been on this journey or are in the middle of that journey. Having a network of others who are trying to or have built a data culture can provide a baseline to your activity, helping you avoid common mistakes, or reassure you that what you are experiencing is normal.

During one of the earlier conferences I attended in my career, I was speaking with other data leaders about some of the challenges I was having, how I wasn't able to get data on the agenda when the business was making strategic decisions that influenced the annual planning, for example. I approached people at the conference to network with and a few who I felt would be somewhat senior in their organizations, based on their job titles. Speaking about my challenges, most of them nodded and told me that this is normal or shared some wise words about persevering, as it will happen. It was surprising but also a relief to know that what I was experiencing was something that others had experienced or were experiencing.

I recall at a networking event organized by a vendor for data leaders, a round table type format, we were discussing the challenges of recruiting and retaining data talent. One of the participants described that they found it hard to retain data talent because of the data team not getting many challenging business problems to solve and that most of the time they were delivering numbers to the business either on an ad hoc basis or in the form of regular reports. Interestingly, several other participants chipped in, echoing the same, that most of their team were engaged in reporting-type activities and the business wasn't challenging them with what they considered the important questions. However, one person did contribute a solution to the discussion, which is something I mentioned earlier in this chapter – get data teams to understand more about the business. This, she said, would allow the data team to understand how the analysis they are doing is related to how the business makes money, grows, saves costs, etc. From this the team can then contribute to these bigger questions in a more proactive way. What these experiences highlighted to me was that the problems and challenges I was facing were not unique to me, and other people may have tried solutions that worked, or did not work. In other instances, I have been given advice which has helped me bypass some mistakes that would have otherwise been made.

Therefore, the importance of building a network cannot be underestimated when you are trying to build a data culture. It ensures that you are connected with like-minded people who are facing similar challenges to you, who can help and advise you when things become challenging. This network doesn't need to be just external, but can, and really should, include internal people, as you never know where helpful information and advice can come from.

This was illustrated on one occasion when I was working with an analytics team within a large agency. The head of the data team, a senior analyst, was struggling on a project where they had to build a simulation model using software that their client had specifically requested. As many of you who work for large corporations will know, getting access to any software not approved by the central IT team is not an easy feat. The process, which is common in most organizations of this scale, is to send a request to the IT support team to have this new piece of software installed on the analyst's laptop/PC. The IT support team then will send their usual response, which is that they don't support this software and an exception can only be made if it has been approved by the relevant person.

This then leads to a cycle of getting approval, sending the relevant approval to the IT support team, and letting them then remotely access your PC to install the software. Once the software has been installed, your analysts go away happy for about two seconds, when they complain that a package or an update the software is requesting can't be installed. So follows another request to the IT support team, who by now have closed the ticket, and you have to raise a new one and explain it all again, get approval again and wait whilst they remote into your PC to install the update or package. This wasn't great for the data analysts in the company in this illustration, as it showed the inflexibility of the organization to facilitate the work that the data team does. They felt no one was championing their work, or understood their specific needs, and that they were left to solve their own problems.

The advice I gave this senior analyst, which I mentioned earlier in this chapter, was to become best friends with the IT departments. From my early days working in the NHS, I had to make several trips to IT support to ask for data applications, such as analytical tools, open-source applications and even plug-ins to be installed. Since these were not organization approved, I needed to get approval to get them to install it. However, after a few visits, IT support coached me to ask my manager to get me admin approval for my PC so I could in future install these applications myself. I didn't know this was an option, but they said that they do allow a select group of people to do this, who they know won't be careless in what they install, and plus there was antivirus/malware software to detect and stop threats.

I only got this advice and support from them because over time I had built a strong relationship with IT support, explaining why I needed applications and what I would be doing with them. I made sure they understood that, in the data space, there are always new tools, many of which are open source, and for different work you may need different applications. I also explained how the work my team and I did impacted business success.

To build a strong data culture in your organization, networking externally and internally can be hugely valuable and also create mutually supporting networks that can be conducive to developing a healthy data culture.

Summary

To start developing a data culture as a data leader you need to start at the top. Make sure that you are engaging with senior leadership regularly and not just periodically. You should also identify a senior sponsor who can represent data at a senior level and keep on the business' radar. In addition, seek stakeholders across the business and get their support, even if they are not direct users of your data analysis. You also need to focus on your team and ensure that they understand the business and how it operates. This will help them deliver better and more relevant analysis.

As a data team, you need to also build trust across the organization. This will help when collaborating with different teams and it will be easier to have your work received. However, never produce any analysis that creates doubt about the data team's capability or the accuracy of the data. Your team should pay attention to detail and always ensure that the numbers they produce are always accurate.

To get started on your data-driven journey you should build an executional road map. This will allow you to identify and deliver quick wins alongside larger projects. It is always better to start small and focus on a single use case than to tackle everything at once. To ensure that the business understands what you have done, train your data analysts to develop the art of storytelling so they can communicate findings in a manner the business will be receptive to.

A data maturity assessment is something that helps the organization understand where they are and how far they need to go to be data-driven, and should be done periodically to baseline the organization. This can help align the organization with their current status and determine how they get to the next stage. Finally, as a data leader, build a network of internal and external peers to validate your thinking and to build out a support network for difficult times.

Reference

Sousa, D A (2011) *How the Brain Learns*, 4th edn, Corwin Press, Thousand Oaks, CA

What to avoid when developing a data culture 5

Building a data culture can be difficult, and even when you have the building blocks in place there is a need to continually ensure that things operate as they should, processes are followed and stakeholders and peers are involved. Like all transformational processes, there is no single end point but a journey where milestones are met and indicators of a healthy data culture emerge, as will be discussed in Chapter 8.

However, to give yourself the best chance of building a strong data culture there can be some pitfalls and mistakes that you can avoid. In this chapter we explore the things you should avoid.

Losing leadership support

I've spoken to several data leaders who have left their organization because the focus on data by senior leadership had waned and they had lost interest in the data initiatives being executed throughout the business. One business leader had built a very good team and had integrated the use of data in the day-to-day activities of the organization; on the whole, it could be said that they had developed a strong data culture. However, their senior sponsor had left the organization owing to ill health and had been replaced by someone new.

Though this new person, when interviewing for the role, assured the data leader that data was important for them and that they would have his full support, once he had joined other priorities had meant that he focused less on data than his predecessor. Owing to this, the senior leadership were not hearing about the great work that the data team were doing on a frequent basis and, as other priorities became more important, backing for data was weakened.

Without strong backing from senior leadership, efforts to develop a data culture can lose momentum and credibility. Leadership commitment is crucial to set the tone and expectations. Whereas before there was a focus on data and the related initiatives, now senior leadership were focused elsewhere. This meant that for this data leader, the budget and support was not there as before, and they struggled to get data back on the company's agenda. Eventually, though, they left as the support from senior leadership had waned and they found it difficult to constantly have to reinforce the data culture they had built. These were small things, from people not following processes to external data being used to make a decision in contradiction to what the internal data was saying. This didn't happen overnight, and, as the data leader explained to me, they just woke up one day and realized that the organization no longer reflected the data culture they had built and they no longer felt a part of it.

Losing the support of senior leadership can happen and often does. For data leaders and data teams, data is integral to what they do. It may not be so critical to other parts of the business. Unless someone is championing the use of data, raising the profile of data initiatives and communicating the success and learning from data on a regular basis to senior leadership, over time other priorities will occupy the senior leadership's agenda in your organization, and some of those priorities may result in actions that weaken the data culture.

An example of this is when I was asked by a company to help them understand what they needed to build an internal data team. This company did have a data team once and over time, owing to cost cutting and on the direction of one of the directors of the company, had outsourced the data team's function to a third-party consultancy. This outsourcing resulted in data being seen by the organization as an arm's length activity, with the consultancy eventually just becoming a service delivery arm of the business. Data and its subsequent results and findings were only used where absolutely needed and that resulted in a very poor data culture. A new CMO had joined the company and I was asked to create a strategy which would see data being brought back in-house. We discussed why he wanted to do this and he said that, when he interviewed for the role, he spoke to a few people in the organization who mentioned how data was used to support decision-making and that the data team were often asked to present the work they had been doing. However, once the team had been outsourced, the regular interactions with the data team became less, as the outsourced team, though delivering on all the analysis, did not really engage with the people in the organization beyond their immediate client. Over time, the senior leadership lost interest in the data as it wasn't as central to the business and was also not visible. This visibility was a key component in the loss of support from senior leadership.

My work there resulted in the onboarding of many of the tasks back in-house and hiring the relevant resources, and though we were able to do this relatively quickly the practices of the organization took much longer to change. Processes were put in place as well as informal engagement mechanisms which allowed the data team to be involved in decision-making across the organization, especially in marketing. The positive was that the new CMO was an advocate for data, and would champion the use of data, as well as replay examples of where using data had significant impact on business objectives in his previous roles.

Whenever I have spoken to senior leadership about the main reason for losing interest in the data initiative, they tell me that it was owing to a handful of factors. The primary reason was that there were other priorities, usually ones that required the business to grow or to cut costs. Though they knew data was part of this equation, there were easier and more direct ways of growing the business or cutting costs, and these just shifted the senior leadership's attention and support away from data. Another reason for lack of support was that data no longer had the focus in the company that it did previously. What they said was that the data team went into a 'business as usual' mode, delivering regular and predictable analysis, with no effort to innovate or experiment to discover new information.

Data leaders and their teams became too fixated on fixing and answering questions to existing problems; they were no longer part of finding future solutions for the company. One other reason that was stated was that, too often, the data team would put up barriers to why something couldn't be done and not offer any solutions. Once all the 'easy' questions are answered, the business inevitably has requests to answer more complex or deeper questions. This requires access to data that the business potentially collects but is not accessible to the data team.

So begins a journey for the data team, where questions cannot be answered because access to data is lacking, getting access to data is a longer process, requiring working with different technology and other teams across the business. What for the data team appears in the first instance to be an easy task spirals into a catalogue of changes and development that goes into months. Whilst waiting for that all to happen, the data team focuses back on business-as-usual and provides 'excuses' for why they can't answer the more complex questions. At some stage people get so frustrated by repeatedly hearing about the problems of accessing data, or lack of data, or quality of data, that they stop asking, looking instead for a third-party agency who can answer the question, even if it is in a different way.

These things can creep up on a data team, especially if they become extremely busy and, over time, the support of the business wanes without the data team realizing before it is too late and bad habits begin to form because the business is not getting what it needs, leading to a poor data culture.

Depending on one key sponsor

My experience of running data initiatives in organizations, large or small, is that you get a lot of traction if you have a senior sponsor for data. However, this I have found can also be an Achilles' heel, especially if too much dependency is placed on that person. I have seen entire data functions fade away when a key sponsor leaves an organization. In one of my early roles, I had a very strong senior sponsor, and with their support I was able to build a team who did work that was used throughout the business. Most senior leaders will eventually move roles, and if that move happens to be with another company, as it was in my case, then you will find, like I did, that the attention data received starts to fade somewhat from the psyche of the organization. This will not be immediate, as others will try to pick up the mantra of being the data sponsor, and in my case I was fortunate that after my senior sponsor had left the organization I received support from another senior leader.

However, as a data team we had become too dependent on our senior sponsor to help us achieve some of the ambitions we had. Now that we did not have that support, we found it much harder. Over time, and this becomes very gradual, budgets for the team either stay flat or are reduced. When someone leaves, their role is either delayed in being filled or not filled at all. Some functions the team did are questioned and even cease as they are beyond the data teams' scope.

With our senior sponsor, why and what we did was part of the history we shared. We didn't need to really connect with other senior leaders as we relied on our sponsor to champion our cause. This then meant we were very exposed once they left, with other senior leaders only aware of what we did but not involved in what we did. Eventually, the team started to get smaller, because the tasks we were asked to do became narrower to what the business felt we should focus on. My manager was eventually replaced with someone new from outside the organization who had their own vision for how to deliver on data.

After a while, I had also moved on and the team that I left behind was only half the size from its peak, and a skeleton operation a few months after. Maybe that suited where the company was at the time, but it did highlight how important it was to not rely too much on one sponsor. It's all too easy during the period you have this sponsor to believe it will always be like this, but I have witnessed subsequently that in other places data cultures begin to erode once key people leave.

In order to build a solid data culture it is essential that, even if you have a key sponsor at the leadership level, you still reach out to other leaders within your organization and include them in the data journey.

Make everyone an ally of data, and show them how the outputs from data can help them directly in the role that they do. This then ensures that if one or more key leaders who sponsored your data initiative leaves, you still have others who value what data can do for the organization and for them specifically, and they will champion the data agenda.

Taking sides

This brings me on to a topic that is hard when, as a data leader, you want to gain support, or recognition, for the work you are doing. You may find it tempting to help colleagues or teams to support, defend or promote a decision by providing data which has been manipulated. After all, if you manipulate the analysis of data, you can present a story that promotes a certain narrative. This becomes especially pertinent when you have a very strong sponsor who is enthusiastic about the organization using data. This empowers the team to do the great work that they want to do, but it also creates a dynamic in the relationship where the data team may feel that they also need to support this sponsor in their decisions and activities in the business.

I've seen data teams be both obvious in their support as well as subtle, and sometimes even unaware that they are taking sides. A negative side effect of this is that others may not or will not be accepting of the findings even when objective work is presented. The wider detrimental effects of this are a data culture that can be toxic, with data being weaponized to drive agendas. The reality is that these cultures manifest themselves as siloed organizations, with different teams using their own data, with systems often owned by the different teams. They also rarely share findings or even the basis for their decision-making. It can even go as far as some teams making a case for their own analysts or analytics team.

As data leaders trying to build a data culture where decisions and actions are based on data, in the short term aligning with a particular team can be useful to execute particular use cases and demonstrate success early on. However, dependence on delivering analytics for a team can lead to unorthodox practices which can lead to wilful misrepresentation of data, whether consciously or unconsciously. Someone once told me that it was 'PR math' – the ability to present the numbers in the best possible light, without even being aware that you were doing it.

Though it may not be the team as a whole who does this, even an individual analyst in the team taking sides can lead to erosion of trust in the whole team and data more widely in the organization. This is particularly true in small data teams, as individual analysts try to find belonging within the organization by aligning themselves with a team or department as the data team is too small to be its own group.

When data analysts are made to feel important by a particular individual or team, their self-esteem is then derived from being seen as important by that team, and their analysis is then influenced by this group membership, with findings of analysis presented to always show the team or department in a positive light. As I have mentioned previously, apart from the obvious ways that data can be manipulated knowingly by analysts to help a team be 'right', it can appear in more subtle forms in a data team's work.

Redefining KPIs

One of the most common requests made to data analysts is to look at the way the KPI was calculated in the first place. This is especially the case when KPIs can be curated to be whatever someone wants them to be. Take for example the KPI of 'returning customers'. A client was tasked with showing an increase in returning customers to the business, so that they could argue that they needed an increase in budget for their CRM team. When you start any type of analysis where terms have been calculated by business rules, you need to understand what these calculations are. In this example, a returning customer was based on the concept of an active customer.

The business definition for an active customer was someone who had transacted in the last 12 months. Therefore, a returning customer was an active customer who had transacted no more than 12 months since their last transaction. Anyone who had not transacted in the last 12 months was considered an inactive customer, and if they transacted after they had become inactive, they were considered a rescued customer. The reason the business differentiated between a returning customer and a rescued customer was that customers who had become inactive were targeted with special offers to 'rescue' them, often at a greater cost than active returning customers.

The client, however, wanted to show that they were doing a great job with their CRM program and needed a larger team and more marketing technology. The data, however, showed that the rate of returning customers was on the decline and at best was actually flat. There was no case to be made for an increase. However, the analyst on the project was asked to increase the window for an active customer from 12 months to 24 months and then look at returning customers. Obviously when they did that, especially if you don't change the methodology or calculation for previous years, returning customers did increase, and in this case more than doubled. Though the analyst argued that the current analysis was not comparative with previous numbers, the head of CRM argued that historically they were looking at returning customers wrong and this new definition was more accurate.

This is not an isolated experience when speaking to many data leaders. Throughout their career a common complaint has been that they have been asked to find numbers that support a viewpoint by redefining the KPIs that are measured and reported on by the organization. A recent example replayed to me by a data leader was that they had been asked to redefine the definition of 'direct traffic' to the site, to show that the editorial team's investments in content are working. The data as it was currently measured and reported on showed that the investment clearly wasn't working, but the editorial team needed to show that it was, and their solution to this was to ask the analytics team to redefine the 'direct traffic' KPI.

Adding business logic

An interesting experience I had of analysts taking sides was burying some business logic into a piece of analysis which no one could understand. Business logic in analysis is applying a conversion to the numbers because the business operates in a certain way. This is often a result of some operating practice which is unique to that business and needs to be reflected in any analysis. This logic then needs to be consistently applied to all analysis to provide a like for like comparison. For a loyalty programme I consulted on, there was a calculation of a short-term effect of campaigns being run and you could calculate this through a short-term campaign based on return on investment (ROI) analysis, using a campaign control group. However, the analytics team had also devised a long-term effect of their loyalty programme and applied a weighting to the short-term ROI to calculate the long-term effect of the loyalty programme.

There is actually nothing wrong with that, as the team had built an econometric model which showed the long-term effect, in this instance two years of the loyalty programme, on sales. However, buried in their calculation was that they compounded the long-term effect for each campaign. So, for example, if the ROI of a campaign A is X, and the long-term effect, in this case two years, is Y, then you would expect that this long-term effect of Y is not just the artefact of solely campaign A, but also of all other campaigns run in that two-year window. However, what the team were doing was for each campaign adding a long-term effect of Y. This meant that if they ran 10 campaigns over the course of two years, instead of including the long-term effect of Y over two years, they were including 10Y over two years.

So obviously the success of the loyalty programme looked great, and the business never questioned or even knew this was occurring. Obscuring numbers with business logic to support a team is quite dangerous, as any ROI calculation by nature can be dissected, and should a new analyst or loyalty programme manager come into role and question why the long-term effect was 10Y instead of Y, then things will begin to unravel very quickly.

Picking and choosing metrics

Often, success can be measured in many ways, and it has been known that people like to only use metrics that show them in a good light. When you have many options to choose from, why wouldn't you choose the ones which show that your team or department is meeting or exceeding its target? Often analysts don't feel empowered to question why certain KPIs are chosen over others and will, without any malicious intent, present only those metrics which show the team in a positive light as opposed to others, equally valid, which do not. If you work with a sales team, you will find that being asked to chop and change how you report on their success is quite common, and KPIs drive their commission or bonuses and so they need the best chance of success, so why not choose the KPI that shows that?

These scenarios occur when the data team is seen mainly as a service delivery unit and not consulted or considered a partner in the decision-making process. This then results in the data team doing what they are told, especially if the organization regards data and the data team as just tools to be used when needed. Often this leads to organizations having conflicting reports, and the ability to learn is hindered as there is no consistency in any analysis and senior management are unsure of whose numbers to trust.

Data leaders and data teams need to be very cautious about taking sides. There is a fine balance between refining an analysis by changing KPIs to show accurately what is happening and manipulating a piece of analysis to show what others want.

Perpetuating silos

A consequence of data teams taking sides is that they exacerbate any divisions that already exist within companies. Where it becomes obvious that data teams are not impartial, other teams may decide to source their own data or even hire their own analysts or get their analytics from third parties. It can even result in teams being wary of the systems that the data team is using and go on to procure their own data and reporting systems.

These divisions perpetuate any silos that may have existed between teams before or even create new ones. This siloed activity doesn't always restrict itself to teams not working together, but also there may be teams who have their own siloed data which is not connected or aligned to the data from other teams. Decisions are then made with partial and siloed data, not giving the business a full or comprehensive view of business performance.

This then erodes trust in the data as those at the top are exposed to competing metrics and can never get a straight answer to often simple questions. This loss of trust can permeate to the data leader and data teams, with senior leadership approving the use of different data systems and even the hiring of separate data analysts for different teams.

In my experience, where divisional silos exist, especially when they have their own siloed data systems or sources, creating a healthy data culture is extremely difficult. Each team believes they have a good data culture through the use of their own data, not understanding that operating in a siloed manner, even if their decision-making is data-driven, makes it difficult to know whether the actions taken are good for the business, even if they are good for the department.

An excessive focus on technology

A consequence of siloed activity is the belief that technology will solve the data problems in an organization. Organizations, when they find themselves unable to nurture a healthy data culture, will often turn to technology as a saviour, believing that bypassing the cultural and human aspect of an organization in its involvement in data would solve the problem.

I once consulted for a very large retailer which believed that deploying a marketing automation system to power their loyalty programme and CRM would make them become data-driven. They spent a lot of time and effort engaging with consulting firms to understand what technology to use, what operating models to adopt and what resources were needed to make this happen. The bulk of the effort went into the technology and the operating model. The consulting firm explained how by using the technology they could essentially build something that would result in what they called a 'lights out' scenario. This was essentially that all business logic would be programmed into the marketing automation system, and then all communications sent to customers would be automated, with the marketing team only needing to build out the assets.

Though a worthy ambition, there was no consideration given to how the marketing team would know what assets to build, no thought given to who would analyse the data and how they would do it. It was assumed that, as the marketing automation system had reporting functionality, the marketing executives would run their own reports and derive the insights which would help them plan and execute marketing campaigns.

What happened in reality was that, soon after the system went live, the marketing team were unable to get the answers they needed from the system, changes in business priorities required the consulting firm to deploy a team of developers to change the logic in the system to reflect the business priorities and the 'lights out' ambition was far from a reality.

To solve some of the reporting issues that the marketing team had, they decided to buy a dashboarding solution that was more intuitive to use. To help the company make changes to the system to reflect new business objectives, an interface was developed on top of the marketing automation tool so someone with limited programming knowledge could make those changes. All and any problems encountered were deemed solvable with a technology solution. My company was brought in by the CRM team to deliver some customer analytics in the form of a recency, frequency, and monetary value (RFM) segmentation, cross-sell and upsell models, and other propensity models, such as churn and reactivation models.

To do our work, we just extracted the data directly from the marketing automation systems database, and built the customer segmentation and predictive models outside the system and then fed the results back in. Even then, there was a desire to automate these customer segmentations and predictive models.

From the outside, what my team and I saw was a company looking to be data-driven through automation and technology and not people. The data was just seen as a fuel for the marketing automation system, there to make it smarter in delivering the right message to the right customer through the right channel. There was no culture of wanting to understand any insights from the data, whether the data may help in wider business decision-making or if the data could be used to innovate new solutions.

The result of relying too much on technology led to the business not being agile. Marketing teams who needed to respond in short time frames were handicapped and would often seek solutions 'outside' the prescribed solution. Manual processes were then also adopted and third-party solutions introduced to the company. This then creates organizational silos, which as discussed previously is never good for a healthy data culture.

Relying on technology to build a data-driven company can only go so far, and you will find that its output will be very narrow. Absolutely, technology is part of the equation in being data-driven, but an excessive focus on technology is not the answer. A balance must be sought. The company we consulted for never did learn that lesson and eventually abandoned one technology for another, hoping that a change in technology would help them achieve their ambition of being data-driven with an automated system. The lack of awareness that an excessive focus on technology can never be the only solution hindered the ability of that company to move forward in developing a strong data culture.

Waiting for perfection

Another key reason why organizations fail at building a strong data culture is that they often wait for things to be perfect. When speaking with Min Bhogaita, he said that often his clients used data quality as an excuse to not do analytics and therefore not to develop a data culture. It is rare to find an organization that has what might be considered perfect data. Even when data is structured and stored in relational databases, with the ability to easily query and return results, the data may still not be perfect.

I have often found that rules and assumptions are coded into many analytical queries across varying organizations to return often simple numbers like total sales, customers and products. This is because the data in the databases may not capture some information, or it captures additional data that needs to be excluded. This requires the business to make a judgement and adjust the data in a way that gets them what they need to operate. However, the goodwill that organizations lend to data initiatives can easily be eroded when data teams or other teams complain that the data is not perfect. Expecting the data to be perfect before doing anything means you never start the journey to being data-driven or informed. Also, while perfect data may seem ideal, it is often elusive and can lead to delays and missed opportunities.

A large problem with this is that collecting perfect data can be a time-consuming process. Waiting for all data to be flawless and complete may cause significant delays in decision-making or execution of data initiatives. In rapidly changing business environments, such delays can lead to missed opportunities or reduced competitiveness. In a sector that is competitive, organizations that can make decisions and take action based on available data, even if it's not perfect, can gain a significant advantage over those that wait for perfection. Others will capitalize on this obsession with perfect data and move ahead, leading to an organization falling behind.

I have also seen that organizations that wait for perfect data are less agile and responsive. In dynamic markets, being able to make quick decisions based on imperfect but robust and accurate data may be more valuable than waiting for perfect data that may never materialize. This is true where marketing campaigns need to be evaluated or where products need to be optimized on a frequent basis. Being able to operate with some reliable and good-quality data, however incomplete, can be advantageous in many instances. Without that approach, opportunities may also be missed because decisions based on good-quality but not perfect data can still yield positive outcomes, while the opportunity cost of inaction can be substantial.

There is also a cost element to making sure you have collected perfect data. This often requires substantial resources in terms of time, money and personnel. Organizations may allocate excessive resources to data collection and validation, which may only create 5 per cent additional value. Also, real-world conditions change constantly. Waiting for perfect data may mean that the information becomes outdated or irrelevant by the time it is available and the associated cost of waiting for it to be perfect increases.

Waiting for perfect data can sometimes be self-defeating in developing a data culture, as the information and insights delivered after having waited for that all-elusive perfect data may not be timely. For some aspects of the business, getting an answer quickly, however rough or indicative it may be, is sometimes better than not getting a number at all or getting it too late because there is an expiry date for that finding. I find this quite typical when working with the PR teams in organizations. Often, they will ask to have a number they can have to share with a publication. Since the publication has a deadline, the number is needed before it goes to print. In these cases, even if the data is not seen as perfect, but you are able to run the analysis on good-quality data which gives you an idea of what the final number will be or is a proxy of the number the PR team is looking for, that is often better than having nothing to share. For most organizations I have worked with, I have found that if we trusted the data, and even if it was not perfect, sharing something that is accurate and makes for a good story embeds the work of the data team strongly in the company. Not being able to be agile and respond with imperfect data can mean teams such as the PR team will bypass the data team in the future and seek their answer elsewhere, even if that answer is just the opinion of someone in the organization.

Finally, waiting for perfection in many cases is not possible, as perfect data may not exist. For example, when we wanted to measure how many unique viewers we had across TV and VoD at ITV, we couldn't wait for BARB, the TV audience measurement system used by the British broadcasting industry to measure TV viewership, to amend its methodology to account for VoD viewing. Plus, even with the best methodology it was never going to be perfect. Therefore, we developed our own methodology to calculate total audience numbers across TV and VoD using the various data sources we had at our disposal as we knew that the perfect data we wanted did not exist.

However imperfect that total audience number was, it still provided valuable insights and opportunities for learning and improvement. Also, perfection in data is often subjective, and data quality standards can vary across different contexts and industries. This subjectivity can introduce uncertainty and disagreements about when data is considered 'perfect'. I have had numerous discussions about the use of cookies and device identification numbers as a means to measure users to websites and mobile over the years. We know that it is not perfect, but it serves as a good proxy and, however imperfect, is a useful source of insights.

Though I wouldn't want to advocate using bad data, waiting for perfection can often stall the beginnings of good data culture in many organizations. There needs to be a balanced approach that acknowledges the limitations of available data while taking measured risks can be more effective than waiting for perfect data. Organizations should carefully consider the trade-offs between data quality, timeliness and resource allocation to make informed decisions.

Lack of quick wins

Often when trying to deliver a data strategy, organizations identify lofty and ambitious projects, which would be transformational. Though it may seem like the right thing to do, as it is often said that you need to get the fundamentals right before you do anything, this building of the fundamentals can take a long time and potentially deliver very few tangible results.

An example is trying to unify your data sources so that all data across the organization is accessible to different systems, allowing for reporting, CRM, CMS and other teams to easily access the data they need to deliver better decisions, more personalized customer experiences or more relevant content. I believe all organizations should be doing this but, as discussed in Chapter 4, even though this may be a strategic project which is core to the organization's data strategy, there needs to be an executional road map which delivers on quick and short projects that deliver tangible value.

Focusing solely on long-term projects without delivering any quick wins can lead to frustration and scepticism among employees, and the leadership may lose interest in the data initiative. Therefore, finding use cases that would deliver quick wins when building your data strategy and developing your executional road map will ensure that the organization stays engaged. Again, what is common when there is a lack of quick wins is some departments may become so impatient in waiting for results or waiting for their use cases to be prioritized that they decide to deliver their data initiative or projects outside the data team's supervision. This is not uncommon as this is where teams, as mentioned previously, will hire their own analysts or turn to a third-party agency or consultancy to deliver on their use cases. Unfortunately, if data initiatives are isolated from the rest of the organization, it creates a divide and limits the integration of data-driven insights into decision-making processes.

Black box analytics

It is tempting to show how smart you, and your team, are as a data leader, and this can lead to building really complex and often obscure models and data outputs. This then usually results in the findings, or the insights generated, being too convoluted to explain, confusing those whom it is meant to inform. Though many of the more complex analysis can be seen as black box, as a data leader you should aim to simplify the complex. This is best done by not using terminology which the business is unlikely to understand when delivering the results, and to keep away from the technical aspects of how you did the analysis. What I found to work best is to take any analysis you or your team have done and see if you can demystify what has been done by using analogies.

Though it may not always be appropriate, when presenting the outcomes of a piece of analysis, especially one that required a slightly complex set of analytical techniques, using analogies has served me well. In meetings I will usually explain a piece of analysis by using a simple example that my audience will understand. For example, in a meeting with a marketing manager for Microsoft, I explained that CRM is like your local shopkeeper. In the morning he sees you when you come to buy a newspaper. He may sometimes see you come in and buy some sweets after work, and at weekend he might see you when you buy some essentials like milk. Then one day he may see you come in to buy milk on a Friday evening. He assumes you have run out early this week, and when you go to pay for it he asks how your family is and then mentions that he has some new sweets which your children may like. Like a CRM system, he is collecting data points and understanding more about you, and when the time is right promotes something that would be of interest to you.

Often, analysts find that they cannot explain things by substituting something complex with an easier to understand example. This is more common amongst analysts who rarely need to justify what they have done and have found that their analysis is just accepted at face value. Therefore, using analogies can serve to translate the complex into something more relatable.

However, when the business is uncertain or unsure of how the analysis was conducted, it becomes sceptical of the outputs. This will be amplified when the results do not align with current expectations and observations. Therefore, being able to explain your analysis becomes a key to reassuring and demystifying the analysis. Where you include assumptions or business logic, be sure to note down why they were included, so that it can be explained to the business why these exceptions are added to the analysis and why they will impact the outputs.

In the data science space, black box analytics is now becoming common with the use of machine learning. Its use to answer every business question can have a negative impact on building a data culture. When the business does not understand exactly what has been done (and with some ML techniques even the analysts have difficulty in explaining how the models work) there is a tendency to brush aside the methodology behind these analyses. Unless, of course, they can prove to demonstrable tangible business value, in which case the business may not care to know as long as it's delivering value. However, even then I have found that some business leaders become slightly nervous relying on the analysis which they do not fully understand and worry that, should the analysts leave, then they have no way of transferring that knowledge to others in the organization. Where possible, try to avoid any analysis that is hard to explain or seems like a black box, where one set of numbers goes in and another set comes out, without any transparency on what has happened to them.

One size does not fit all

I've always had supportive bosses who championed the work my team and I have done. But it is inevitable that you will encounter bosses who have a different way of working with data. In one of my roles I had a new boss who didn't agree with the way I had set up the data team and wanted it to be exactly like the team he had in his previous role. He believed that he could replicate what he had at his previous company. This is a common mistake leaders, and also data leaders, make when they come into a new organization. Though much of what they have done previously will be applicable, how it is implemented and even executed needs to take into consideration the specific practices, values and organizational culture of their current organization.

Even if you are hired because the business wants you to replicate the success you had at your previous place, unless the cultural nuances of the current business are taken into consideration then it's a recipe for failure. I left a few months into my new boss's tenure, and he also left a few months afterwards, as the organization operated in a way that didn't suit his own operating style. In another instance, I was asked to assist a new data leader to execute their data strategy. They had been very successful being a senior data leader at a similar organization but in a different country. Much of what they set out in their strategy worked well, but there were some elements which did not align with the culture of their new organization. As such, they found that some teams and even departments could not align with the strategy and some of the practices they wanted to introduce went against how the organization operated. Owing to this, they met some resistance, and when you are trying to build a data culture, you need support.

Though it is good to apply what you have learnt elsewhere to any new organization you join, assuming that one size fits all is a mistake. It's easy to fall into this trap, especially if you felt that developing a data culture in one place was successful and that replicating the formula will work elsewhere. After my time at ITV, I did some consulting for STV to help them with their data strategy. It was an interesting situation, as one would expect that STV was just a smaller version of ITV. STV is Scotland's equivalent to ITV in England and Wales. It shows many of the shows that ITV aired, but also had its own shows. However, working with STV I realized that many of the things that I implemented at ITV were just not applicable at STV. As a smaller entity compared with ITV, STV operated very differently, as did their people, and this I needed to take into consideration when creating the data strategy for them.

Later, when I worked setting up data teams in other countries, especially in Asia, understanding the general cultural difference as well as organizational practices heavily influenced how I set up data teams in those locations. Setting up teams in Prague was very different to setting up teams in Jakarta, and setting up teams in Dhaka was very different from setting up teams in the UK. But even within the UK, where I have spent the majority of my career, different types of organizations need to be approached very differently. An example I witnessed was when a very competent data leader met resistance when they came from a data analytics background into an organization that already had its own data culture, formed over years from having a research department. These companies, you will find, are very comfortable with the findings they receive from research studies and are able to make very informed strategic decisions based on these studies. As a data leader, you may be surprised that very important strategic decisions are made with findings from focus groups which only consist of three or four participants.

Coming into a company with a well-established research department will require you to be a partner in enhancing an existing data culture, as opposed to coming to an organization without a research department or one with a weak research operation. When there is a strong research department operating for years, such as there will be in many fast-moving consumer goods (FMCGs), consumer-packaged goods (CPGs) and automotive manufacturers, adapting to that culture and taking what is good can work well. However, if you come in to abolish the existing data culture and enforce a new one, based solely on data analytics and ignore the value that data from primary research brings to the table, not only will you meet with resistance but you will also miss out on an opportunity to widen your exposure to different data sources.

Finally, even within your own company, a one-size-fits-all approach does not work. Every department and team has different needs and levels of data maturity. Avoid applying the same approach uniformly, and instead tailor your strategy to each group's needs.

Ignoring governance

Something that can put a stop to a strong data culture taking hold in an organization is ignoring or having weak data governance. How you decide on what processes and procedures you have in place which govern or influence how you use data can play a significant role in developing a healthy data culture. It's often tempting in the early days of setting up a data function and evolving a data culture to be flexible and agile, and play slightly loosely with rules and regulations to get things done. However, as the company matures, without strong data governance in place people within the organization won't know what they can and should be doing.

Take something like data privacy. Regulations around these areas are always changing and will also vary from country to country. Therefore, as part of your data strategy and wider business strategy, you should have in place processes that allow you to determine how you adhere to data privacy regulations. This will then dictate your data accessibility policies. Once you have determined what can be done with the data you collect, you can then decide who needs access to this data and also who the data can be shared with.

Data ownership and data security then would need to be considered, as there will need to be a data owner who is responsible for the data collected and what is done with it, as well as when it should no longer be available. Data security would then provide the mechanism by which data owners allow accessibility.

Finally, as part of governance you will need to consider data ethics, as neglecting ethical considerations can lead to data breaches, distrust and legal issues. Implementing a robust data governance framework which has clear ethical guidelines on what can and cannot be done with the data will lead to transparency in how the data is used, trust and clear rules on what can and cannot be shared, internally and externally.

Overlooking data literacy

One of the many things that I do when coaching data analysts, whether senior or junior, is to make them realize that what they may find easy to understand is not true for others. Assuming that everyone understands data concepts can lead to confusion and misinterpretation. This can be an overlooked area and I have found it to be a big source of misunderstanding within the organization and can quickly lead to the erosion of trust.

Therefore, prioritize data literacy training to ensure that employees can effectively work with data. As mentioned in previous chapters, data literacy initiatives do not solely have to be formal, but can be informal through the ongoing interaction between the data team and the wider business. In order to understand whether you as a data analyst are being understood, listen for feedback. It is tempting to ignore feedback, but if you do you can miss where someone is telling you that they don't understand what you have presented, or they have interpreted what you have presented very differently. Establish channels for feedback and actively listen to concerns. This allows mistakes to be avoided that could negatively impact the data culture and the pursuit of data initiatives within the organization.

What makes a good data leader

6

How to build and nurture a team, and the types of people to recruit

Setting up a data function within an organization starts from getting it right with the person who will run the team. Often, when a company starts the journey they have the luxury of hiring a data leader to come in and set the agenda, create the data strategy, and execute a data-driven approach. Even where a data function exists, even if it is nascent, it will be necessary to hire a data leader or identify one from within.

I've worked with many data leaders, some good and great, others not so. What you observe is that, like all leaders, there are certain traits, characteristics and behaviours you see which indicate qualities that would be desirable in a data leader, including those who would cultivate a data culture.

What makes a good data leader

As mentioned in the previous chapter, one size does not fit all organizations when developing a data culture, and different data leaders may thrive in different organizations. However, in my discussions with data leaders, they mentioned the common attributes of data expertise, spanning both the scientific and technical aspects of the role, passion for the commercial side of the business, liking the entrepreneurship part of it, seeing the bigger picture and having great management and leadership skills. These also are the common attributes I've seen in my experience working with data leaders.

A data leader should always keep an eye on the bigger picture. As a data leader you should be able to put the analysis your team and you do into a relevant context for the business. This allows the business to understand how it can use that data for decision-making. It is not enough just to present the results of any analysis and leave it to the business or different departments to make sense of the findings. By being keen to provide the business context, the data leader ensures that data is also relevant in its use. If you detach what the findings of any analysis mean for the business then it becomes something that's nice to have but not essential. Keeping an eye on what the business wants to achieve and delivering analysis which helps them do that is key for any data leader.

The most obvious skill that people should look for in a data leader is data expertise. A good data leader should possess a solid understanding of data concepts, tools and technologies. They must be knowledgeable about data management, analysis and visualization. This may seem obvious, but you often find data leaders emerge from either very narrow data domains, such as business intelligence or customer analytics, or from ancillary domains such as strategy, finance or even product. Though they may prove to be great data leaders, it is always worth checking that they have a broad understanding of the entire data ecosystem. This is often overlooked as those hiring data leaders will not necessarily know the entire data ecosystem themselves and rely on those they are hiring or promoting from within the organization to define what that is.

Without a significant depth of expertise in data, the data leader will find it difficult to command the respect of their team, but also be unable to realize the data vision of the organization, as they will themselves not have a full understanding of what is possible with data. In one of my more recent engagements, a data leader was promoted from within the organization. This person had significant domain expertise and was technically very impressive. However, they did not have the strategic mindset that the organization needed to move forward. What happened was that this person, once promoted to the data leadership role, just continued to deliver in the same manner as they did before, which was restricted to sending analysis in the form of a report for every request made to the team, instead of partnering with the organization to understand what they wanted to achieve and whether they were asking the right questions of the data. They did not even consider other approaches to using the data and exploring different technical and analytical solutions in answering business questions. Though this is what the business needed at this stage of data maturity to fully realize its data strategy and develop a strong data culture, they had hired someone who was good at what they had done in the past and not necessarily what they needed for the future.

Most exceptional data leaders can span both the scientific and technical aspects of the role as well as speak the language of the business. The data landscape is constantly evolving. Good data leaders need to be adaptable and open to exploring new tools and techniques, fostering an environment of innovation. I have found that very good data leaders are adept at identifying business problems that can be addressed with data. They guide their teams in formulating hypotheses and designing data-driven solutions. Good data leaders are also very outcome-focused. They measure the success of data initiatives based on their impact on the organization's goals, rather than just technical achievements or how they would prefer to do it. So, for example, when an organization states it wants access to data, the data leader needs to evaluate whether this means having a self-serve business intelligence system, more analysts or more training for the different teams. They need to evaluate what the organization wants to achieve instead of just deploying what they know or how they prefer to do things. To achieve this they should engage in continuous learning as data and technology are always evolving. I have always advised data leaders to continually be on a learning path and stay updated with the latest trends and advancements in the data field. This requires an investment of time to achieve and is definitely worthwhile.

Another aspect of a good data leader is their passion about the commercial side of the role. This is something I have always found engaging about my roles as a data leader. I've always been passionate about how the analysis that is being done by my team impacts the business's commercial side. It's something that Adam Wright, Chief Data Officer at Oodle Car Finance, mentioned when I discussed with him what makes a good data leader. He said it is someone who is interested in how the business drives commercial success and will align data activities and initiatives that would contribute to that success. This doesn't need to be limited to just building business cases for data initiatives, but thinking wider in identifying opportunities that would drive growth, save costs and enhance competitiveness.

Another related thing that Adam and I discussed was that data leaders should like business and the entrepreneurship part of it. This got me thinking about how in a field like data there are well established disciplines like business intelligence and reporting, customer analytics and propensity modelling. But new areas are always emerging, such as the application of computer vision and generative AI. Data leaders who want to create a strong data culture need to have a love of business, understand what makes a company successful, stay competitive and plan for the future, but also love entrepreneurship, involving a need to innovate and stay on top of the latest progress made in the area.

This also includes change management skills. It is not enough just to have ideas and expect the business to adopt them. Developing a data culture often involves change and data leaders need to effectively manage resistance, communicate the benefits of change and guide the organization through the transition. This is a skill that I have seen data leaders shy away from, as they see it as confrontational. However, with the right training in change management or just going on general leadership courses, data leaders can develop these skills which can make them far more effective.

To be more effective you also need to be everywhere as a data leader. Being visible is a key attribute of being a data leader. Even if they need to spend time behind the screen working on analytical problems, or are introverted in nature, they have to be visible within the organization and even wider. In my discussion with Min Bhogaita, we talked about how data leaders who are not natural business leaders should seek training from the organization to develop business skills. Min's observation was that introverts probably do make good data leaders, as he ascribes to them having less of an ego, and so are willing for their team to also shine. However, on the negative side they do not seek to be a partner to the business and this is key if they want to avoid some of the pitfalls mentioned in Chapter 5.

A strong data leader is one who is championing the use of data, presenting and speaking internally and externally about the success, challenges and failures. They should be able to transcend traditional organizational barriers by being able to break down silos and foster partnerships between different groups with different goals, mindsets, levels of understanding and ways of working. Data initiatives often involve cross-functional collaboration. A strong data leader can work effectively with teams from different departments, influencing them to embrace data-driven practices. However, Stephen Kinsella warns that good data leaders are usually good at what they do and then the business becomes dependent on them, which then means you want to deliver more and more, and that can then lead to burnout.

Finally, like all leaders, a data leader must also have excellent leadership skills. They should be able to identify, develop and retain talent, motivate and empathize with team members, set clear goals and hold the team accountable. What I have found is that effective data leaders empower their team members by providing opportunities for growth and learning. They mentor their team to enhance data skills and develop a culture of continuous improvement. They have resilience and patience with their team and the wider organization, something that I had to learn after spending three years doing a PhD, where I was working on my own. It was a solo journey, whereas a data leader's journey is one of leading from the front. The journey to a data-driven culture can be challenging. Data leaders should remain patient and resilient in the face of setbacks and delays.

This leads on to something I always tell others about what a data leader does. A data leader is a mediator. When people have differing views on how to do things, armed with data the data leader must play a mediating role, listening to both sides, presenting the data in an objective manner and then mediating a solution. I have spent a lot of time in meetings mediating between different individuals, teams and departments. Even when I was working for an agency, some of my clients would take me along to their internal meetings to serve as a neutral and objective voice.

How to build a team

These attributes all contribute to being a strong data leader, but one of the hardest parts of being a data leader is actually building your team. There may be occasions when you will be promoted to a data leader role, and fall comfortably into your new strategic role. You may choose to keep things much the same without taking responsibility for the execution of the strategy – a sort of armchair data leader. I have encountered these data leaders who work as thought leaders in their organization, providing advice and consulting but not actually doing any of the executional work.

However, when being asked to create a data-driven organization, you need to step beyond your strategic comfort zone and immerse yourself in the world of implementation and application.

One of your first tasks will be to hire data analysts, to create a team who can execute your data strategy. When looking to hire that first data analyst, the inevitable question arises of what type of analysts should you hire. From the outside, it may seem that all analysts are the same. But for those of us working in the data space we know that data analysts come in a variety of forms. In addition, in my experience with non-data leaders there is an expectation that a single data analyst can perform all the data analytical tasks for that organization.

Sometimes this is true, as the organization may not know what it wants and therefore what that one data analyst delivers becomes sufficient and all-encompassing for the organization. You don't know what you don't know. However, as a data leader, you should be aware that to deliver on a vision of being a data-driven organization and to develop a strong data culture requires hiring for the current need and then growing the team and skillset as you branch into other areas of the data strategy and executional road map.

If your executional road map requires the development of reports and dashboards in the first instance, before you get to more complicated analytical tasks, then it might not be wise to hire a very senior data analyst or even data scientist as it might be only in 12 months or later that they would expect to be delivering predictive models. Hiring a data analyst for the current task ensures that their skills and expectations match what the organization and you as a data leader will require of them.

I have spoken to many senior data analysts and data scientists who have been unhappy in their role, as they were hired to do advanced analytical tasks, but ended up doing standard reporting. Though there is absolutely nothing wrong with a senior data analyst or data scientist doing this as part of their role, if it were their entire role it would demotivate them and they would think about leaving.

I have even hired data resources for future tasks that did not materialize for many months and that skilled resource was tasked with analytical activities which were far too junior and basic for them. Some analysts will accept the current situation as long as you as a data leader can get them to buy into the strategic vision, and assure them, as well as demonstrate, that what they are doing currently will only be temporary, and they will move on to more interesting and challenging tasks. You also need to have a plan to hire more junior resources to take over the more basic tasks like reporting and basic analytical tasks, and communicate as well as be seen to action this plan.

In the next chapter I will discuss how, as a data leader, reporting is a key component of developing a strong data culture. Although the task may be seen by many analysts as too basic or not challenging enough, it is an essential data activity all organizations need to adopt. Therefore, most data analysts know and have experience of delivering reporting in organizations. Still, after a while they may grow tired of just delivering reporting and discontent could grow in the team. When you think that this may be happening, as a data leader you need to engage proactively with the business to identify more advanced use cases that the team can engage with. In a discussion with Stephen, he mentioned that he even asks his analysts to come up with two or three use cases that he could take to the business and get signed off so the team could do some advanced analytical activities.

Data leaders, however, are faced with a dilemma when building a data team, in that the basics need to be in place before more advanced use cases are addressed. However, starting a team with a junior resource can lead to its own challenges. The first thing to evaluate as a data leader moving into a new role is how much you want to get your hands dirty. If you are a hands-on data leader who can still see the bigger picture but doesn't mind or even loves getting involved in the delivery, then hiring a junior data analyst is fine, as you can step in and do some of the more complex tasks, such as creating data pipelines or statistical analysis, related to fundamental activities.

The junior data analyst will also probably grow much faster as they are stretched to deliver reporting and analysis as well as other analytical tasks on their own. At the same time, they will have access to you as a data leader to either directly assist or guide them in finding solutions. It is unlikely they will get bored too quickly as most things will be new to them and the intricacies and challenges of delivering reports regularly and accurately will keep them interested for at least a year or more, by which time you would have executed more use cases, ideally hired another data analyst and introduced a variety of data analytical tasks into the team.

However, initially hiring a junior data analyst has its drawbacks in that if your involvement in the delivery becomes time-consuming then the data strategy gets neglected. In this case you may find that you struggle to exhibit the characteristics of a good data leader discussed previously and some of the potential challenges discussed in Chapter 5 could occur. So unless you believe that your involvement in delivery will be minimal and most of it can be done by the junior data analyst then it's probably not a good idea to hire a junior data analyst initially. Check your executional road map and pick out the first 12 months of activity, and determine whether they could largely be done by a junior data analyst with minimal assistance from yourself. If not, then you will probably need someone with experience.

As mentioned, hiring too senior a data analyst can also be problematic, and you may end up delaying the decision because you can't decide what level of data analyst to hire. So my advice and that of other data leaders I spoke to when writing this book is to hire for attitude. Obviously look for their technical skills, but then go beyond that to see how they would approach the role. You are looking for pragmatic individuals who understand that nothing is perfect and that working in an imperfect situation is often necessary. Lara Izlan from ITV also mentioned hiring people who are comfortable with debate and dissent.

As you grow the team you are not going to agree on everything, and if it is just you, the data leader and the data analyst then you need to be comfortable with them asking you the 'why' questions and challenging you to qualify your decisions. The reason for this is, as you grow the team, you want to avoid the first hire becoming someone who accommodates requests and potentially takes sides or is easily persuaded to re-interpret results to suit agendas.

The bitter reality with any hiring is that you never know how someone will work out. But my recommendation would be to hire someone senior who has the right attitude to the role, appreciating that they may be asked to do tasks that they consider to be basic, and often work unsupervised, or with very minimal guidance, and just need to get on with the job.

The three things I look for when hiring my first data analyst for the team are:

1 **Are they proactive?** In the interview stage, design questions that help you to understand whether the person is proactive. As mentioned, they need to work with minimal supervision, but they also need to be able to proactively get on with tasks. This expands to building relationships with stakeholders, working with different teams and discovering and implementing solutions on their own. You can get a sense of this during the interview, if they talk about who they regularly worked with in their previous roles. How they've approached problems, any proactive work they have done without being asked and how they identified the opportunity are all key elements to understanding their suitability to the role.

2 **Are they practitioners of data?** My experience of hiring analysts, especially in the era of low code analytical tools, is that many will make claims for what they have done or are able to do, but are unable to do so in practice – they can 'talk the talk' but not 'walk the walk'. I have interviewed individuals who claimed to have built

predictive models but when quizzed about what statistical tests or approaches they used, they had no idea or respond with generic answers like 'I used machine learning'. Someone who can 'walk the walk' will be able to discuss the details as opposed to just answering questions very vaguely. So when interviewing, ask them to explain in detail the approaches they took, the details and rationale behind the statistics they used and also some of the failings they've had. A practitioner of data should have detailed answers to these questions.

3 **Do they have great PR skills?** Finally, as this will be your first hire, you will both be ambassadors for the data team and the data proposition within the organization. As discussed in earlier chapters, the behaviours that the data team exhibit reflect the data culture being grown within the organization. So the person you hire needs to be able to go out there and talk about the work of the data team, and not just merely describe it, but also sell it in, shining a light on its success and framing the failures as learning opportunities. When interviewing, ensure that you leave time for them to exhibit their communication skills, and get them to discuss how they've managed to communicate their and their team's work, how they've convinced people who might have been resistant and how often they did this. I always advise the hiring manager to look out for how enthusiastically they discuss past projects – even if the projects themselves are not interesting, showing passion in discussing them shows they have the foundations of great PR skills.

How to nurture and grow a team

There is probably no single way of nurturing and growing a data team, and each data leader should discover what works for them. In my experience, I have given each of my analysts opportunities to learn new skills, ensured there were sufficient challenges in the work-load so they were stretched but not stressed and allowed the opportunity and power to be heard.

Lara Izlan and I discussed this topic for the book and she also mentioned that you need to foster the type of environment that allows your analysts' voices to be heard. She explained that as a data leader you need to be transparent with your team on what you are trying to achieve and open about your role with your direct reports. This led to us discussing how, when your team know about the targets you and the team have been set as well as those of the wider department and organization, it is much easier to create the type of environment where data analysts feel they can speak. Understanding the extent of what you and the team can influence and how decisions made by senior leadership impact you and the team also fosters this type of environment where analysts feel they can contribute to discussions.

When you are growing the team, it's important that even during the recruitment phase that you explain the vision you have for the data team and for data within the organization. Data analysts can have differing views about what it means to be a data-driven organization. This expectation, if not addressed early, can lead to differing opinions within the team and lead to a conflicting data culture where the vision for data is not shared. If that occurs within the data team, then it's inevitable that it will resonate throughout the organization.

I worked with a very senior data analyst at an organization who did not agree with the businesses vision of being data-driven, which mainly included the data team providing retrospective analysis to support decision-making. This organization was run by very creative product people who did not believe that data should or could play a role in the creation of ideas and concepts, and they stated the aim of data in their business strategy was to understand the performance of the products, the associated marketing for those products and also the decisions made so that future decisions would be informed by what was learnt. The senior data analyst believed that this meant that the organization just wanted to use data as a crutch to support decisions already made.

In my discussion with the senior leaders within that organization, I could understand why they had decided that, and though they could not see how data could be involved in the creative process they acknowledged that data was important for them to evaluate their ideas and concepts post execution. The senior data analyst, however, felt that some of their creative ideas could be generated from analysing the concepts themselves. His ideas included analysing the images, the copy, and even the discussions which were had about the ideas and products using the latest in machine learning, natural language processing and computer vision techniques.

The business just couldn't see how this would be useful and though they listened and entertained his ideas, it never really went anywhere. Therefore, there was this undercurrent of dissatisfaction from the data team, which I witnessed in almost every one of their weekly meetings, which I had the privilege to sit in on. I could clearly see how the analysts were passionate about the possibilities of data within their organization, but the business was unable to grasp the applications of these ideas.

This situation led to the senior data analyst being disengaged from meetings where the business tried to involve the data team in many of the decision-making processes. As they did not share the same vision about the use of data and the data team could not convince or get the buy-in from the business, it resulted in a stalemate. This was reflected in the data culture, where clearly the team would deliver outputs as a mechanical process and be passive when responding to business questions, but what was very damaging to the data culture was their dismissiveness of any new data initiatives announced by the business, believing that it was just a talking point and not something the business would ever do. In the current climate, data analysts have options, with the demand for 'good' data analysts exceeding available resources. Min and I discussed how hard it is to recruit and retain good data analysts. Once they have been hired you have to make sure to keep them and make them more valuable to the organization. We discussed the need to try to find ways to give analysts the limelight so they feel recognized and valued. We also discussed the need to provide training on the softer skills like storytelling, as when given a choice on what they want to learn data analysts choose technical courses, believing it makes them more valuable.

I also picked this subject up with Abs Owdud, who added that data analysts should also be taught consulting skills, as often data analysts do play the role of internal consultants. He also mentioned that, as a data leader, you should set an example of what you expect from your data analysts, and the best way to do that is to show them, so take them along with you to your presentations and meeting, open up those opportunities for them, and show them how to promote a positive data culture.

The other thing that I believe is important when growing a data team is that you build a sense of team. I discussed this with Adam who said he would watch out for difficult people when growing and nurturing a team, as no matter how good they are as a data analyst, they can make the environment uncomfortable for the others. He also mentioned that you should build a team where your average data analyst fits in and you provide a route for promotion and development. Interestingly, he also said that the team retains the team. It's something that both he and I, as well as other data leaders I have spoken to, mention, that when they stay, they all stay, but when one leaves the rest start leaving. There will always be a team ecosystem, and that needs to be maintained.

To maintain that ecosystem, Adam discussed the need to have the right balance of skills in the team, create mechanisms for them to interact, either in person when in the office or virtually every day by instigating daily stand-up meetings. It's important to ensure that the data leader is someone who other data analysts want to follow as well as just generally hiring good people. When discussing with Julie Screech how to nurture a team, she said that it was easy for data analysts to be good enough and that led to a deterioration in the team and the data culture in the organization. Therefore, fill your team with people who are persistently curious. Adam mentioned that is why there is a bias to hiring people who are academically oriented as they exhibit this trait of curiosity.

When nurturing a data team, the overwhelming message I got from all of the data leaders I interviewed for this book was the importance of creating a culture of openness from the start. It was felt by these data leaders that where there is an openness within the team, it is easier for the team to discuss issues more openly. Being part of the data team is never easy; from heavy workloads to unrealistic expectations, the data team needs to deliver on time and highly accurately. Having an environment where these things can be discussed within the team allows the data analysts to feel that, even if things don't get better, at least someone is listening.

In all the teams I have run, I have always allowed my data analysts to feel they are safe in discussing their challenges, and that the organization respects that at times it can be challenging, and they would not be judged. This is not something that happens by accident – it needs to be cultivated.

Other things to consider when growing and nurturing a data team:

- **Clearly define the roles and responsibilities of each team member.** This even goes as far as defining their seniority. In the early days, when you have two or three data analysts, they may report to you directly, but then as the team grows and you need to create a hierarchy, junior members of the team may resent having to report to someone else instead of directly to you. Getting this clear from the outset, and defining everyone's role, helps to keep the team aligned and content. The other element I always take into consideration is to recognize the strengths of each team member and assign tasks accordingly. Not only does this maximize productivity and job satisfaction, but it also shows that I have listened to what my data analysts want to do and reflected that in the tasks that have been assigned to them.

- **Set clear performance expectations, goals and KPIs for each team member.** Align their work with the organization's objectives. This really helps the team understand how their work is contributing to the company's success. Often, data analysts can't see how what they do has an impact, so make this explicit in their performance plan. It is also a great way to show them the career progression plan within the organization, allowing the data analysts to feel that they have room for growth in the organization.

- **Source candidates with a mix of technical expertise and domain knowledge.** As you grow the team, there is a temptation and even tendency to recruit data analysts who are very similar. To avoid this you could advertise your open roles in different places, or use different recruiters, or even proactively seek out candidates with different backgrounds. One of the things I do once I have a team with a strong analytical skill set is to hire people who come from unconventional academic backgrounds like languages, communication and humanities. What I look for in those individuals is a passion for data and a track record of delivering results. The team can teach them the technical skills, but their approach and mindset cannot be taught. Build a diverse team that brings a wide range of perspectives and experiences. Diversity fosters creativity and leads to more well-rounded solutions.

- **Encourage a culture of teamwork and collaboration.** When you go from one or two analysts to a larger team, what you don't want is a series of highly talented individuals working on their own. Create opportunities for team members to share insights, knowledge, and best practices. Also, facilitate collaboration with other departments. Data insights often have the most impact when they're integrated into various aspects of the business.

- **Invest in training and professional development.** The data landscape changes so quickly and data analysts sometimes feel that they are not getting exposure to the latest data technologies, approaches or innovations. A way to mitigate or address that is to invest in training and professional development to keep the team's skills up to date with the latest tools and techniques in the data field. Beyond formal training, I also encourage my team to stay updated with the latest trends in data science, analytics and technology. As a data leader, you can demonstrate this by forwarding interesting articles to the team, showing that you are taking time out of your day to stay up to date on the latest in the data space, and this should keep your team at the forefront of the field. I've seen teams instigate 'lunch and learns', weekly email round-ups of what's new and even a 'learning and sharing' channel on Slack or Microsoft Teams.

- **Plan how to provide guidance, mentorship, and leadership.** One of the things I have noted about data leaders, and even I have been guilty of this, is that once the team gets to a certain size, or the work the team is doing is getting noticed and used across the business, the data leader becomes preoccupied with attending meetings with other business leaders and becoming less available to the team. Be conscious of this and put in place a plan for how you will provide guidance, mentorship and leadership support to help team members grow in their roles. This could involve empowering them to take ownership of projects and objectives.

- **Ensure your team has the necessary tools.** Interestingly, one of the biggest complaints I hear from data analysts is that they don't have access to the appropriate tools to do their work properly. Whether that be a powerful laptop or particular software, you need to equip your team with the necessary tools and resources, such as data analysis platforms, databases and cloud services, to enable efficient work.

- **Have an entrepreneurship mindset.** To be a good data leader, we discussed earlier that having a business and entrepreneurship mindset is helpful. This trait should also be encouraged in the team. Allow your team to experiment and innovate. Encourage them to explore new methods, technologies and approaches to solving data-related challenges.

- **Acknowledge achievements.** If you are the type of data leader who gets satisfaction from doing a great job, you might find yourself failing to recognize and reward your team. I have had to consciously focus on this aspect in my role as a data leader. Acknowledge and reward team members' achievements and contributions. If you fail to celebrate achievements, the team can feel that their work is being taken for granted. So celebrate project milestones, successful analyses and other accomplishments. This reinforces a positive team culture, and recognition of good work boosts morale and motivates the team, even if it is a weekly 'shout out' to someone who has done something above and beyond.

- **Provide constructive and regular feedback.** As a data leader, you should also provide regular feedback. Constructive feedback helps team members improve their skills and performance. Regular feedback sessions promote growth and help you to identify any issues before they occur. This is an area that I and many data leaders neglect, sometimes because of not wanting to be seen as being critical, but often because the pace of delivery means that it's hard to just pause and reflect on what someone has done to provide them with constructive feedback.

- **Encourage ethical data use.** Coming from a social science background, running my research idea through an ethics committee was a natural part of the process. Then moving to the NHS, this was still something I had to do. But when coming to the private sector, I was struck by how little consideration is given to data ethics. Companies routinely collect data from customers, and pre-GDPR without even their consent, but rarely did I encounter a situation where a discussion was had of why we should collect this data and what we would do with it. No one seemed to be concerned about the impact of collecting and using this data on customers and consumers. Even now, the only reason we have a debate on why we collect data and what we do with it, is if it impacts the customer journey and reduces some form of conversion. In my experience there is no customer data advocate in an organization, and so as a data leader I would assume that role. I therefore always instil a sense of responsibility for ethical data usage and security in my team. I emphasize the importance of maintaining privacy and complying with regulations. With new data protection and privacy laws coming out, this job has become much easier, but nonetheless, when growing a team, each person needs to know how to use data ethically and responsibly.

Types of analysts to hire for the rest of your team

When writing this section of the chapter I didn't want to fall into the trap of describing all data analysts in a stereotypical way, which I am known to accuse others of doing. However, as a data leader, if you need to grow a team and need to hire more data analysts, what should you look for to complement the ones you already have? The obvious factor is that they have analytical skills. This includes, depending on the level of analyst, some basic or advanced statistical knowledge. This is a fundamental skill set and if data analysts don't have that, then you will struggle to get them up to speed. If it's a junior or entry level role, you wouldn't expect much statistical knowledge but you would still expect a basic understanding of statistical concepts.

Where I have ignored my instinct and given someone a chance who wasn't strong in statistics, I have found that it was a struggle to get them to pick up simple analytical tasks quickly. At a minimum I expect them to have at least done well at mathematics at high school level. Even if they didn't study statistics at university or didn't go to university, having been on a short course shows they would be able to deal with the fundamental analysis required of the role.

The next skill I look for, or that they would have an aptitude to learn, is a programming language. For entry level roles they probably don't need to have experience of those tools, but middle to senior levels would be expected to have those skills. You would need to look for proficiency in a data analysis tool such as Excel or SQL, and a statistical programming language like Python or R, which are essential for data manipulation and analysis. However, even for junior or entry level roles I would check to see if they show any evidence of attempting to use a programming language, even if it is for personal projects.

I would also look for their natural style of presenting data. For instance, during the interview stage you could give them a small data set and ask them to create a presentation, representing the data in the best way possible to answer a particular business question. As part of that exercise, you can assess their problem-solving skills as well as their communications skills. If people are good at them naturally then they do typically grow to be very good data analysts.

The exercise should also highlight their time management skills, but this is something you should dig deeper into during the interview. When working on a data problem, data analysts need to understand what the cost of finding out the answer is against the value of that knowledge. I discuss this in more detail in Chapter 7, as it's a concept that Stephen uses when training his data analysts, and also when explaining to the business how he prioritizes all of their requests. This means that data analysts should exhibit very good time management skills.

One of the key aspects I look for in a data analyst is attention to detail. Data analysis requires meticulous attention to detail to ensure data accuracy and to spot inconsistencies or anomalies. If data analysts cannot pay attention to detail then you need to wonder if they would pay attention to the important things. An anecdote that Stephen shared with me was that in the 1970s pop bands would make strict and particular requests of the venue hosting their performance. For one band, the request was for green M&Ms in an American football helmet. When the band turned up they would look for the green M&Ms in a football helmet and if they found that request had been fulfilled, then they could be reassured that the speakers would work. What was demonstrated here was that someone who cared about what seemed like a trivial request, a small detail, could be trusted with more important things. As a data analyst, if you cannot get the basics right, such as correct labelling of charts and graphs or consistency in decimal places for all your numbers, then there would be some doubt as to whether you have got the main numbers right.

Something we have discussed has been finding data analysts with a curiosity and learning mindset. A good data analyst is curious, eager to learn new techniques and stay up to date with the latest trends. Therefore, when interviewing, ask their opinion about something that is currently trending in the data space or something that is topical. I often find that those with a keen interest in data will have an opinion, even if it's one you do not agree with. This leads on to critical thinking. I used to believe that having an undergraduate degree was a benchmark of critical thinking skills, but recently I've realized that has not always been the case. I try to introduce a discussion point during the interview to explore their critical thinking capabilities. This is a tough one, but you should have some questions on their ability to evaluate the validity of data sources, methodologies, and assumptions in their analyses. Maybe get them to discuss a project they had worked on and evaluate their critical thinking skills when talking about the challenges and limitations.

Finally, when you hire a data analyst whether it's your first analytical hire or subsequent ones, ask them what they know about the business they are applying to work for. I am always surprised by the number of people who I have interviewed who had no domain knowledge, and couldn't describe how the business operates, how it makes money, or even if it had offices nationally or internationally. You need someone who has an interest in how you operate as a business, as it helps them to understand how what they do contributes to this.

Even though I have stated what I would look for in an analyst, and did not want to fall into that trap, it's worth noting that analysts who have the positive attributes mentioned will prove to be a positive contribution to the team and the organization, and help foster a strong data culture.

Beware the rock-star analyst

Going back to your first hire, hiring someone too junior doesn't always work out well, unless you as the data leader want to be seriously hands on. Though most organizations will want to hire someone at a senior level who has a few years' experience, and is able to technically do what is necessary, they need to beware of the rock-star analyst. In my experience of having started several data teams at various companies as well as assisting others in setting up their data teams, I have come across analysts, who in the first year or so, become a 'rock star' in the organization. They come in and almost immediately start to add value.

Not only are they technically amazing, but they are also really good at engaging with stakeholders. In the beginning, the company may think they have hit the jackpot, as this data analyst goes from problem to problem answering an array of previously unsolved questions. The different teams will love working with them, they go beyond what is expected of them and start to take on extra responsibilities.

In one of the teams I created, I had one of these rock-star analysts. He was much loved by the organization, working diligently and often long hours to get the job done. From a leadership point of view, this is perfect and you leave them to it. However, once he had left, I discovered that he was doing the work of others in the company, and took on far more of a wider remit than he should have, which explained why the other teams loved him, but also why he worked such long hours.

Having a rock-star analyst as your first hire can pose some serious issues. In my experience there are three main problems that arise with these types of analysts. The first is that they start to mould the data culture in their image. That is to say, they create processes, procedures and even solutions based on how they have been taught or how they have learnt things. This may not be a bad thing, but alternative solutions are often not explored, and as they are seen as the expert, people are unwilling to challenge them. This also becomes more of a problem when you begin to hire other analysts to join the team, and the rock-star analyst finds it difficult to work with others or the other analysts find it difficult to work with the idiosyncratic ways and processes of this particular analyst. Another potential issue is, if they leave, how they created their ways of working can leave with them. The main reason for this is that the processes and procedures are in the analyst's head and not shared for others to understand and work within the constraints of.

Secondly, being the sole analyst for a while and being very much loved and in demand, they now have to share this, and having to share work and attention can be hard for them. Other analysts may find that unless they do it exactly as the rock-star analyst did, then the work is dismissed or the rock-star analyst takes over and does the work in the way that they want to do it. They may not delegate any tasks and instead want to do everything themselves, as well as being critical of others' work. This then results in the new analysts being demoralized, and conflict arises if the new analysts are on the same level, or the new analysts will leave.

Thirdly and the most common, is that they outgrow the role too quickly and either want to be promoted or will seek to move on. Now, the sensible choice is sometimes to allow them to move on. Once you have hired additional data analysts, you will find that you don't have a dependency on a single analyst and you are comfortable if they choose to leave. The risk, however, is the body of knowledge and network they have built within your organization would be lost if they leave. So, you would ideally like them to stay.

So, the challenge is, where do you place them? If they are good, you find that you don't want to ask them to leave, especially since the company has become used to all the amazing stuff they have done. So you have a couple of choices. If they are not good at managing others, and generally in organizations managing others is linked to promotion and higher pay, then you must create a route for them where they can still rise up the ranks but not have to manage others. It's more difficult if they are also someone who doesn't like to work with others. From experience, I generally find that these rock-star analysts find it hard to manage others, but that doesn't preclude them from being good team players.

The other option is to carve out data analytical activities that they would be good at and can run in isolation of the team. This is not ideal, but you will find that when rolling out your data strategy there will be several activities on the executional road map that lend themselves to being standalone projects that they could work on. By delivering these ideally high-value projects, you can make a business case to have them promoted to a more senior role and also provide the associated pay rise.

However, sometimes these analysts have an ego and so are neither a good manager of people nor a good team player. For one of the consulting projects I did for an agency, I came across a rock-star analyst who the agency found was not good working with other analysts. From the praise they received, it would be assumed that they were doing a good job. However, the head of strategy who they reported to was having problems growing the team as they ventured to win more clients. The head of strategy explained that the analyst was not a good manager of people, judging by the number of analysts reporting to them quitting, but they were also not generally a team player.

My remit was to understand the needs of the agency and expand the data team, including ways of working as well as other aspects of growing a data practice in an agency. In my discussions with the head of strategy, I found out that this data analyst had come in as the first permanent data analyst to the agency, after a series of freelance or temporary data analysts had come and gone. This analyst worked closely with all the different client teams from the outset, answering those difficult data questions that needed answers, helping clients solve reporting issues and generally being insightful. This led to the agency relying on this individual, with the individual feeling valued in return, and therefore going out of their way to continue to do a great job. However, over time, as most agencies want to do, they wanted to expand their analytical capabilities and so wanted to recruit another analyst to support their rock-star analyst.

Initially things went well with the first hire, but after a couple of months the new hire was beginning to complain that the work they did was taken, redone and presented to the clients without their knowledge, or at the last minute they were asked to hand over a piece of work as it wasn't done 'properly'. The culmination of these controlling behaviours led the new analyst to leave, and then another was hired, who left within a month. After the third new hire left, I was referred by a mutual acquaintance to help this agency grow its analytical team.

In my discussions with the wider agency team, mainly the account team, I found they had no issues with their rock-star analyst. Rather it was that other analysts they hired in the past who were perceived as an issue. They clearly didn't want to lose him and he didn't want to leave. The solution here was that the organization had a data culture revolving around an individual who was generally very good and did all the right things. So rather than change the environment to be a more inclusive data culture from the outside by implementing processes and practices, I decided to instigate change by coaching the analyst to help them understand how they could grow their team and still maintain the data culture they wanted. These things don't happen overnight, and much of it is explaining how different people do things differently and that is fine, and that there is no single way of doing something. Even in something so concrete as data, there is a huge element of art and judgement involved, and they needed to appreciate that.

The other element of the coaching was to help them identify what they excel at, and in this analyst's case they excelled at solving new business questions and challenges, so we worked on how they could delegate the routine reporting and analysis to new, potentially junior analysts, and they could focus on the more complex issues. This then freed them up to do what they liked doing, as well as have others assist them with all the other things that needed doing. However, analysts like this one very rarely make good managers, and it's best to have the other analysts report to someone else, which we did in this case.

Whilst writing this chapter, I did a quick search on LinkedIn to find out whether that particular rock-star analyst was still in role and if the team was more than just one person, and I was pleased to see that they were still in role, and there were two other analysts also at the agency. However, my sense is that the additional analysts were brought in owing to new client wins and that these new analysts will be working separately from this rock-star analyst.

One of the things I have discovered in my experience of starting data teams and speaking with other data leaders who have also started data teams is that you can't really avoid these types of analysts. Though they tend to have an ego, there is no denying that, without their skills, expertise and enthusiasm, getting significant progress in the early days is not possible for just the data leader to do with someone who is just good enough. You need this type of person and if you actively avoid recruiting them you tend to have other issues. These can range from needing to recruit multiple people from day one to recruiting senior resource who seem not to have an ego, but then you find that they do not want to do the basics, as they applied to the role as a senior and are only interested doing the analytical activities mentioned in the job description and vision for the data strategy.

So, on the one hand, you can't and shouldn't avoid hiring rock-star analysts, but on the other hand, if you do, getting things off the ground is much harder. In the several instances I have hired these rock-star analysts for my own team, I have had two types of discussions. The first is that they want to be promoted too quickly and not show development in the non-technical skills, in which case when I point this out, they don't acknowledge it and then choose to look elsewhere and leave. The other discussion is where the analyst and I will have a frank talk about their future at the company. We can both see them outgrowing the role, but also that they, and often I, don't see a role for them in the new evolved team. We then agree an exit strategy and I have on many occasions helped them find their new role.

The humble hero

As you grow out your data team, there is always a certain type of analyst I call the humble hero who will eventually be part of most teams. When interviewing several data leaders for this book a common attribute they mentioned about data analysts who you want in your teams is that of being humble. So that's why I decided to name this type of analyst the humble hero. This analyst is one who will be the backbone of every data team, diligently working on all requests that come their way, solving problems proactively and generally producing robust and consistent work.

The reason I refer to them as the humble hero is that they would never seek out recognition or ask to be rewarded for the work they do. Instead, they gain satisfaction in doing a great job. However, that doesn't mean that they don't need recognition or reward. Since these heroes don't ask, they are often overlooked, and if they are not occasionally appreciated for the work that they do, the first sign of their dissatisfaction will be when they have resigned. At that point, you have lost a great analyst, as they've decided that their current organization doesn't align with their values and ambitions and have decided to move on.

When I've spoken to these humble heroes about why they leave, it's rarely because they find the work hard, boring or even predictable. It's mainly because they don't agree with the data culture of the organization and the vision for data. Part of that misalignment is also to do with not receiving recognition and reward for the hard work that they do, as they believe that an organization with a good data culture would reward its data people. It's unfortunate that you first hear about their dissatisfaction when they resign, and often owing to their humble attributes it's hard to win them back.

I've failed in a few of these instances, especially when I've accelerated the growth of the data strategy and not stayed close to my team. In these instances, I just assumed that these humble heroes who worked without complaint would know that I was appreciative of their efforts, and when the opportunity arose I would speak with them about their future at the company and how to get them promoted. But the time never came, and also, being busy, I didn't think it was a priority. I would only be reminded when these humble heroes produced another great piece of work, and I would mention in passing or in a team meeting that we should have a catch up.

One humble hero I lost was an extremely sad occurrence, as I was speaking with my senior leadership about expanding their role and busy trying to get sign-off and budget for them to be promoted. But in large organizations these things can take time, and I didn't want to promise them anything until I had secured the promotion for them. However, before I could get a decision on the promotion the humble hero resigned, and even when I explained that I was battling hard for them to get a promotion, they had emotionally checked out. When someone does that, it's hard to win them back, as they have already pictured themselves somewhere else.

It's sometimes hard to notice these humble heroes as they diligently go about their tasks, but you should recognize the good work they do. It's worth taking them aside after they produce or present a great piece of analysis and reassure them that their work is being appreciated, not just by you as the data leader, but also by the wider organization. Then make plans for them to be recognized and rewarded appropriately.

The trusted lieutenant

For all data leaders, the journey to developing a data culture can be lonely. You will often find yourself in an organization and amongst leadership peers where you are the only one who understands the potential of data, and are the lone voice championing the cause. However, with the need to ensure that the team is delivering value and working with the business to get buy-in and adoption, you could find yourself stretched and on the way to burn out.

This is where having someone within the team who you can trust to take on some of your responsibilities is key. When you are growing and nurturing a data team, you should by instinct look to identify and nurture your successor. Many data leaders I have spoken to have mentioned that as they have ambitions to grow, and potentially even leave their current organization for a larger role, they don't want to just leave the organization with no one to take the helm and carry on the good work. They discussed how they will always look to see who would be best to succeed them. In my career as a data leader I have always managed to find some trusted lieutenants, and this has helped me immensely in being successful in instilling a strong and healthy data culture in an organization. This person didn't need to be an exact replica, but someone who had the potential to lead the team and continue to foster a healthy data culture. You will find that these individuals are the ones who you can trust to deliver.

If you cannot find them amongst your current team, then when you recruit your next senior hire you should be actively looking for someone who has the capability to step up and lead the team in your absence, whether that be temporary when you are busy or on leave, or permanently if you decide to move on.

I've had examples of both. In one of my roles, I hired a data analyst who I noticed was very good at solving a whole host of problems. In this organization, the use of data was a fairly new concept and so there were many challenges. From amongst the team, I found myself turning to this one individual when I needed something to be solved and delivered. Over time, it became natural that I made them my de facto deputy and would rely on them to lead when I was not around. They also took to this role naturally, so it made sense to eventually promote them into that role.

The other example was having to hire someone to lead the team. This is a delicate one; if you get it wrong you disrupt the hard work of growing and nurturing your existing team. When I recruit for this role directly I look for someone who has great people skills but is also respected as a data analyst. The other main thing is that there is chemistry between the two of you, as you will need to work together. This connection allows you both to be aligned on what you want to achieve, but for them to be comfortable to challenge you and even propose alternative approaches.

As a data leader, to be good, you have to acknowledge that you cannot do everything on your own. If you are also given the remit to build, grow and nurture a team, you should take advantage of working with others who will share your vision for a data-driven organization and developing a strong and healthy data culture. Utilizing your team is your greatest asset. Beyond the technology, your team will be the ones who ultimately deliver your data strategy. Building and growing a team is never easy, but finding the right people to be part of your team can make a huge difference.

Processes, change management and behavioural change

7

Early in my career I had the fortune to work with a group of very impressive management consultants from one of the 'big four' firms. Up until working with them, I didn't really understand what they did, especially outside their auditing businesses. A friend worked for one of them when I was still doing my PhD. The description he gave of his workload seemed to consist mainly of looking at data in Microsoft Excel and helping write Microsoft PowerPoint slides. Though he didn't like much of what he did, he enjoyed going into companies and having an impact. The project I was working on with these management consultants was to introduce a new data platform into an organization. The consultants I worked with were primarily there to ensure that the processes were in place so that people knew how to use this new platform. They referred to this as the 'target operating model'. From what I could understand, they were trying to ensure that people changed their behaviour. With this new data platform in place, they created processes that required people to behave in a new way, and they believed that people would naturally behave in the way they expected just based on introducing these new processes. The end result was a PowerPoint deck and a series of documents that were handed over to my managers. They also did a big presentation, which was primarily to state that the project was officially handed over and that the processes were now in place for us to use the platform.

In my old role as a PhD student, I would probably have taken an experimental approach to what they did, exploring different ways to get people to change their behaviour. For example, I might have looked at past research or conducted an experiment where I tested different approaches that I hypothesized would change behaviour. I might have even taken a model like 'The theory of planned behavior' (Ajzen, 1991) and tried to design an intervention to see if that resulted in the desired behaviour change. However, what I saw from the consultants was the creation of a document, which included processes which were designed based on a target operating model, or an ideal way of working, and then an expectation that people would do exactly as asked. These were based on interviews with the business stakeholders and so did reflect some realities of what people do now and what they needed to do in the future. There was some consideration to edge cases or exceptions. However, there was not much discussion on what would happen if the process didn't work for some people or if some people didn't want to work in that way. Nor was there discussion on how new people would know how to behave if they were not part of the creation of the target operating model.

I moved on to a new role, so I never discovered whether people adopted the target operating model, but I did encounter this situation in many other organizations, where behaviour change was imposed from top down and people were expected to go along with it. I guess in a work environment, the power dynamics mean that if directives are coming from the top for ways of working to change, then people have no choice but to change. However, when these directives or instructions are coming from other departments, often from peers or colleagues, what is the motivation to change?

Take, for example, information security. Often, we are asked to make sure we don't share passwords, write them down, give others our security pass to get in and out of the building, or save data to our personal laptops or storage media. We all know what the rules are, but when faced with some obstacle or barrier to getting our work done, we might try to bypass these instructions. Unless mandated by senior leadership, with accompanying repercussions, these security practices do not really change behaviours. I learnt a lot about that from Flavius Plesu, a former Chief Information Security Officer (CISO) and currently founder and CEO of OutThink, a cyber security human risk management platform for CISOs. He discussed how annual security awareness training with a quiz at the end is supposed to make employees behave more securely. However, he never witnessed them actually doing so. He also mentioned that organizations often see employees as the problem, with processes and procedures in place to stop them being a security risk. Instead, they should be seen as an asset in developing a stronger security culture in the organization. He believed that a new way of training employees was needed, something more targeted and personalized, appreciating the differences in individuals and delivering content that works for them. Changing human behaviour is hard and so he left his former role as a CISO to create a platform that tackles this challenge in the information security space by applying behaviour change models in the information security space.

In my experience, to change behaviour, especially when creating a strong data culture, the data team needs to change organizational practices by being part of that change, while at the same time also introducing practices which overtly and explicitly introduce the use of data to the organization.

If you look at theories of behaviour change, such as 'The theory of planned behavior' (Ajzen, 1991), behaviours are influenced by intentions, which are determined by three factors: attitudes, subjective norms and perceived behavioural control. It is also possible for external factors to directly force or prevent behaviours, regardless of the intention. This depends on the degree to which a behaviour is actually controlled by the individual, and the degree to which perceived behavioural control is an accurate measure of actual behavioural control.

Therefore, for people to want to become data-driven, they need to have the right intention. Actions are based on intentions. So, unless an organization has the right intention of using data to drive commercial success and growth, then it is unlikely to adopt the behaviours needed for developing a strong data culture. If the intention of the organization is not grounded in being data-driven and using data for the benefit of the business, its employees, partners and customers, then no matter what the actions the individuals engage in, there is no chance of the organization getting closer to realizing the value of data. In turn that means there is nothing from which a data culture can emerge. It's in essence an organization giving lip service to data.

Even in today's climate where big data, machine learning and AI are on the brink of revolutionizing the way organizations and even society as a whole approach the world of work, some companies still only give lip service to data.

As Ajzen explains, 'Intentions are assumed to capture the motivational factors that influence behaviour; they are indications of how hard people are willing to try, of how much of an effort they are planning to exert, in order to perform the behaviour. As a general rule, the stronger the intention to engage in a behaviour, the more likely should be its performance' (Ajzen, 1991, p. 181). Therefore, to build a strong data culture, the intention amongst individuals within the organization must be one of believing that they can be a data-driven organization.

So what drives this intention? As mentioned earlier, according to the theory of planned behaviour, intentions are determined by three variables (Brookes, 2023):

1 **Personal attitudes:** This is our attitude towards a particular behaviour. It is the sum of all our knowledge, attitudes and prejudices, positive and negative, that we think of when we consider the behaviour. So, when individuals in an organization use data, there needs to be a question of why they are using it. Is it because they believe that they have to be seen to use data as they need something to rely on if things go wrong? Is it because, if there are questions about why they took a particular decision, they can refer to the data? Or is it because they actually believe that data can make a difference in their role and for their organization?

2 **Subjective norms:** This considers how we view the ideas of other people about a specific behaviour. Does the individual use data because their peers and competition are using data and they don't want to be seen as ignorant? Or is it because using data is the normative behaviour in the company and their industry, and they see it as part of what they do?

3 Perceived behavioural control: This is the extent to which we believe we can control our own behaviour. This depends on our perception of internal factors, such as our own ability and determination, and external factors, such as the resources and support available to us. Brookes argues that our perception of behavioural control has two effects. Firstly, it affects our intentions to behave in a certain way, i.e., the more control we think we have over our behaviour, the stronger our intention to perform it becomes. Secondly, it affects our behaviour directly in that if we perceive that we have a high level of control, we will try harder and longer to succeed.

Developing a data culture requires changing people's behaviours, and this can only be done if they have the right intentions. As explained by the theory of planned behaviour, individuals need to have the right attitude towards data, believe it is something that others would approve of and think that they have control over doing it.

As you can see, the theory of planned behaviour can serve as a start to developing a framework for a target operating model for creating a data culture. You want people to believe that using data for decision-making and being data-driven is the right thing to do, that others are doing it and your organization has it in its control to do this. To start with, it requires something to change and if you as the data leader have been tasked with delivering that change, then ideally you would start with yourself and your data team.

Start with your data team

If you want the organization to change so that they start to use data as part of its operating model, then as a data leader you should start with your team. An important element of building a data culture is that those who are most visible are also seen to be a representation of that culture. Now this doesn't mean that they are the physical manifestation of the data culture. They don't have to be perfect and do the right thing all the time when it comes to using data, but they should have the right intentions and attitudes about data used in their organization. They should also believe that this is something the organization can achieve and is what their competition is most likely doing. Finally, the data team needs to exhibit the relevant data-driven behaviours.

When I hire data analysts or walk into an existing team, I usually discuss with each person how they believe data is having an impact in their current or past organization. I usually seek out their attitudes to the work they are doing. Are they just running analysis for the sake of running analysis, because they have been told to do so, or do they really believe that what they are doing will and does make a difference? I also explore their role in making that difference, how involved they are in becoming part of the change and actively working towards making the organization data-driven, by exemplifying data-driven decision-making in their work and challenging poor data practices. I also seek to understand how much they are contributors of a good data culture as opposed to bystanders being dragged along by others.

Stephen Kinsella explained how he had a process of questions that allowed for his data analysts to be more in control of what analysis they do and less likely to be just there to answer questions on request. To achieve this, he needed his data analysts to become more curious and interested in why the business is asking the question. Therefore, the process he created was a way of getting his data analysts to ask a series of questions of the person requesting the analysis. This allowed the analyst to be proactive in responding to business questions, exploring and challenging the why. It allowed them to not just engage with the request in a procedural way as just a cog in a system that delivers analysis. Stephen asks his data analysts to consider the following:

- Do I understand the question being asked?
  - If no, ask the requester to spell it out.
    - They may have communicated it poorly.
    - Also, clarify the use of buzzwords and define macro terms such as engagement, traffic, success and performance.

- Do I have the data required to answer the question?
  - o If not, can I get it either by collecting that data (e.g. adding tracking to my website to collect it) or can I buy/get that data from second or third parties?
    - − Assess the cost/benefit of doing this.
- Then ask the requester to quantify the value of the question.
  - o What will they do with this analysis that will deliver the business's objectives and KPIs?
  - o Their response should help you determine the priority of this request.
- Then think about what techniques you need to use to analyse this data, e.g. reporting, modelling, feature engineering, etc.
- Determine whether you have the tools to do the analysis.
- Then think about how the output will manifest itself.
  - o What is the best way to represent this information?

Stephen says that data analysts often want to show how good they are by producing lots of graphs and charts. However, sometimes all that the person asking wants is just a number, a table or a simple line chart showing the results of the analysis. That is what the data analyst needs to communicate.

Though not all data analysts may be self-aware enough to ask these questions, in order to develop a strong data culture analysts need to be partners in the business when delivering. Stephen explained that these questions allowed both the data analysts and the person requesting the analysis to think about what they have asked. If the requester cannot articulate why they need the analysis and what they will do with the analysis, the data analysts should be able to help them delve deeper into what the business challenge, problem or question is and then help them formulate the analytical request.

As a data leader, you need to ensure that the analysis your team does adds value. Often you can be delegated to a support function which responds to requests on demand, and be subservient to a team or department. How the data team is treated is hugely dependent on how the data leader positions the team, and part of that is how you approach their coaching and mentoring. If you put things in place that allow your data analysts to be business partners, helping the business drive value from data, then that influences how the rest of the business perceives and treats the data team. The way the data team is treated reflects on the data culture being developed within the organization.

Where the data analyst doesn't take a proactive and intelligent approach to answering the questions asked of them, then data will always be seen as something to use when needed and something that supports existing decision-making. My approach is to coach my team on what it means to be data-driven and how to create a strong and positive data culture. This means that your data analysts should not just perform their analytical tasks but also take an active role in promoting data-driven practices within your organization. This should overlap with what you look for when hiring data analysts when you are growing and nurturing a team, as it is those attributes that translate into the behaviours and practice that your data analysts will exhibit.

Social psychologists would describe this as the dynamic interplay between individuals and the organizations they inhabit. Data analysts play a key role in shaping the collective psyche of an organization, through the actions and behaviours that influence not only the technical aspects of data utilization, but also the very fabric of an organization's culture.

I always tell my teams that one of their main roles as a data analyst is to be advocates for data-driven decision-making. I emphasize that, within an organization, individuals within different teams and departments will be taking cues from those they perceive as credible and knowledgeable. Often that is the data analysts, who they see as a source of data expertise, and so they have the opportunity to wield a profound influence on their colleagues. This is one of the reasons why rock-star analysts have a huge impact in an organization. Their presence as data experts in the company, especially early in the company's data journey, influences how data is perceived and how representatives of data are seen as data partners and models of how data should be used. Through their advocacy of data-driven decision-making, they trigger a process of normative influence, where the individuals from other teams and departments will depend on the data analysts to set the benchmark of how to be data-driven.

This process begins with data analysts encouraging colleagues to validate their decisions with data. They will also be able to share their own views with their colleagues about what the business should do based on the data they have access to. I have been in meetings many times, where I have been asked by the rest of the attendees to aid in coming to a decision, because they believed that my views and opinions would be based on the facts and not be swayed by rhetoric or office politics. Data analysts need to be perceived by the business as using data as a rational, evidence-based approach to decision-making. If data analysts do this consistently, then others in the organization, in their quest for social approval and adherence to group norms, are increasingly inclined to follow suit.

Therefore, I coach and encourage my teams to lead by example. If they consistently incorporate data into their own decision-making processes, and become role models for their colleagues, then others will know what being data-driven looks like. However, there is a caveat to this and that is that data analysts shouldn't operate in secrecy. They need to be transparent when they make a decision or voice an opinion, by referencing the data they have based that decision or opinion on. If they use a data source such as a report or piece of analysis, they should also make that information available to the wider business. Restricting access to information as a way of maintaining relevance and power can be hugely detrimental to a data team and the long-term fostering of a healthy data culture. In being transparent and open, they foster a culture of trust and cooperation, where colleagues feel valued and respected, and thus are more likely to reciprocate by utilizing data responsibly.

However, not all colleagues will be technically minded and some will find it difficult to interpret the data, and rely on the data analyst to do so. Therefore, data analysts need to be ambassadors for data, bridging the gap between the data and non-technical teams. This can be achieved by collaborating with non-technical teams and fostering a sense of unity and shared goals. Positive interactions with the data team and subsequently with data will lead to increased trust and a reduction in any scepticism about the use of data and its usefulness. By addressing the needs and challenges of non-technical departments, data analysts create a culture where the boundaries between these groups blur, and information flows more freely, thus enhancing the organization's collective intelligence.

This should also be complemented by nurturing data literacy within an organization. I tell my data analysts that they sometimes need to be educators. They need to find their style to facilitate the acquisition of data literacy among their non-technical colleagues. Later in this chapter, I will discuss one of the techniques I have developed to build out institutional wisdom, which can be facilitated by the data team, but then continued independently of them. I explain to my data teams that, through observing how the data team uses and disseminates data and its findings, an avenue is provided for individuals across the organization to observe, imitate and interact with data-driven practices. This results in a learning environment where individuals gain confidence in their ability to engage with data and contribute to maintaining a healthy data culture.

One of the ways that data analysts can help other teams use data confidently and improve their data literacy is to use clear and concise visuals that are easy to interpret. Complex graphs and charts are off-putting and do not generally make it easy for non-data personnel to understand what the data is supposed to tell them. To improve the data literacy of an organization, the data team needs to ensure that the organization learns through direct experience of observing and then modelling the outputs of the data team. For those who do not operate in the data space, their first learning experience of using data will be from those who are perceived to be the experts.

Finally, for an organization to feel comfortable with using data, they need to know that the data they are using is of good quality, reliable and consistent. To achieve this, as a data leader you need to facilitate the socialization of data governance. What I mean by this is that data governance should not be seen by the business as something that the data team or a specific data governance person is responsible for. There needs to be processes in place which allow the entire organization to play a role.

This can manifest itself in how data is collected. For example, when forms are created or used by the organization, there needs to be a process to be followed. When collecting customer profile data, does first name and surname need to be collected in two different fields or one field, is title always asked, is gender required and how important is it to consistently collect date of birth? Allowing the teams responsible for collecting this data or teams who utilize this data to be part of creating the framework for how it is collected, and then empowering them with reports, enables these teams to take ownership of the process. By demonstrating the quality and consistency of customer profile data, these teams start to take responsibility and even proactively ensure that data governance around customer profile data is adhered to.

When the organization begins to incorporate data governance principles into ways of working, then this socializes data governance within an organization and allows the organization to develop a healthy data culture. It also allows the organization to start the journey of building and developing institutional wisdom, where what has been learnt and why things are done the way they are, is passed down through teams and between teams without the need for formal knowledge transfer mechanisms.

Building data intuition

When I was working as a senior data analyst, I worked for an organization that would send daily emails which contained a few key metrics or KPIs relevant to each team. They called them flash reports, and one thing I noticed was that after a while I could instinctively identify whether a number in the reports looked wrong. Over time, I began to know what normal looked like and when something didn't look quite right I could sense it. For example, the daily visitors to the website were pretty much the same during the week and roughly halved during the weekend.

Whenever I saw a flash report with a number that did not represent what I was expecting to see, I would know that something was wrong. My belief is that, as humans, we have an instinct when something is not right. We get this feeling in the pit of our stomach. My theory for this is that we don't consciously process all the information we pick up through our senses; a lot of it is unconsciously processed, and therefore our brain will only consciously process information when something looks wrong or out of the ordinary. So, to alert us that something looks wrong or out of the ordinary we have a feeling that something is wrong, rather than analysing all the information consciously to identify what is wrong. From an evolutionary perspective, our ancestors probably survived by being able to quickly identify when something was wrong in their surroundings. They knew when something didn't seem right. For example, when things were too quiet or they saw the shape of a dangerous animal nearby, or a rustling in the distance, they instinctively knew that danger was probably nearby. The brain would process a lot of information about its surrounding from what it collected through the eyes and ears. However, it was not capable of consciously processing all of that information all of the time. Instead, it would likely build out a picture of normality for its surroundings and then when something did not look normal, it would alert us through making us anxious or scared.

Now if the brain had to do this consciously every time it would need to process all that information, match it against safe and unsafe scenarios and then make a judgement. This would require us to engage with System 2 as described by Daniel Kahneman (2011), whereas most of our decision-making is done by System 1. Daniel Kahneman explains that System 1 thinking is a near-instantaneous process; it happens automatically, intuitively, and with little effort. It's driven by instinct and our experiences. System 2 thinking is slower and requires more effort. It is conscious and logical. Therefore, if we used System 2 to make all our judgement, then by the time we made a decision, the danger in the form of a wild animal would likely be upon us and it would be too late to escape. Rather, this information would be processed in System 1, and we would 'feel' the danger based on feeling anxious or getting an intuition that something is wrong. We wouldn't need to consciously process this to react, but later on System 2 may kick in to help us understand why you perceived the situation to be dangerous, but in the moment you just need to survive.

This evolutionary ability for our ancestors to understand when something is wrong probably occurred through operant conditioning (Skinner, 1948). When going about their business, our ancestors probably were originally in a heightened state of awareness when exposed to a novel environment. But as the senses became familiar with the environment and they were not eaten by wild animals or exposed to another form of danger, they could relax. However, when they encountered a novel situation that deviated from the norm they probably went into a heightened state of awareness, and depending on the outcome, e.g. the presence or absence of danger, the brain would learn whether that novel situation was safe or not. Now, when things are not normal, it's not like we do a rational calculation of the situation. Rather, the senses send information to the brain which then uses the way we feel to get us ready to fight or take flight.

These evolutionary human abilities, designed to help our ancestors stay alive, have also helped us to adapt to modern life and even the world of data. With my background in psychology, my tenure of managing teams has also been a lifelong series of experiments to see if I can make them better and more effective data teams. One thing I was interested in doing was ensuring that they knew when the numbers were wrong before the organization did, so that they could be on top of it or even answer it before the questions came raining down.

If you work in data you will know that there are many reasons why the data could be wrong or seem wrong:

- The systems that collect the data failed. For example, it is common for website tracking to fail when site changes are made and the tracking was not tested post change.
- The systems that store that data failed to update. For example, extract, transform, load (ETL) process or data pipelines failed to fully or partially load the data.
- An event happened. For example, a successful marketing campaign exponentially increased revenue or customer numbers beyond what we typically see.
- External events led to a fall in numbers, such as competitors offering a discount.

If analysts don't know what good looks like, then they won't know what bad looks like. So I used what I had learnt personally from receiving daily flash reports to 'train' analysts to instinctively know when the numbers looked wrong. I asked them to set up some daily reports which focused on three to five key metrics. These could be revenue, number of customers/visitors, volume, leads, etc. These reports were then emailed to every data analyst daily so they arrived as the first thing in their inbox.

Unlike senior management or other teams who look at these numbers and then decide if any action needs to be taken, for my data analysts the objective was to become familiar with the numbers. So, if the company gets 200,000 visitors to the website, or has sales of £45,000 each day on average, then over time the data analyst picks up this pattern, and yes it can move up or down by 5 to 10 per cent, but the analyst will start picking up this variation too. If one day the report showed they have 100,000 visitors or 250,000 visitors, they should instinctively know that something is wrong. They should know that even before registering what the actual numbers are – the numbers should just look wrong to them. Data analysts I have trained using this method, when they check the flash reports each day, build this ability to sense when a number looks wrong. However, it doesn't always work and analysts do miss when numbers are wrong or the process of seeing these daily flash reports does not build in the intuition for data. In those instances, you need to work with the data analysts to find a method that works for them. For some it could be that they run a particular report each morning, as the process of running the numbers rather than reading an email might work better.

If, on the whole, the data team can identify when a number looks wrong before the rest of the business does, then if they proactively contact the business, explain that the number could potentially be wrong and they are investigating, it shows to the business that the data team really cares about the numbers and reports it sends out. This reinforces a strong data culture, as an organization can only be data-driven if the data is accurate.

The other benefit of building this data intuition is that data analysts become very familiar with the data. So when someone asks what the average daily sales or daily visitors are, then after seeing the numbers (almost) every day in flash reports, your data analysts should be able to just reel those numbers off from memory. Whenever, I am working with a client, one of the first things I ask is to be included in their regular reporting cadence. If they don't have one, then I will ask their data analysts to give me access to their reporting solution or access to historical reports, so that I can become familiar with their numbers and eventually be able to spot when something looks wrong.

This is something that you should instil in your data analysts. They may not know the exact sales number yesterday or last month, but for the core KPIs that they regularly analyse and report on for the business, they should know approximately what it is. Therefore, in a meeting or presentation, they should know whether a number looks right, without having to go and check. It's the sign of a good data analyst and contributes significantly to creating a positive data culture.

Building institutional wisdom

Once you have ensured that your data team is promoting a positive data culture and exhibiting the behaviours that shows the rest of the organization how to use data to be data-driven, you need to work with the different individuals and teams in your organization to promote the beliefs, attitudes, behaviours and practices that instil a strong data culture in the wider business and endure in the long term.

If you are new to the organization or have been promoted to a data leader role, you should spend some time in the early days and weeks understanding how the business currently uses data. In this exercise you are trying to determine whether the use of data across the business is independent of the data team having to encourage or convince the business to use it. We discussed this in some detail in Chapter 4; however, here I want to provide a practical example of how I achieved this. This approach is something that ingrains itself in how a company uses data and builds institutional wisdom within the organization. However, before that I wanted to pick up on something that Stephen shared with me. He created a formula for how to get the organization to think about the value of what they ask and how it can be achieved. The reason I want to mention this, is that many requests that are made to the data team are unrealistic or not well thought-out.

In too many organizations, I have had people come up to me and say, 'Can I have an insight about X, Y or Z?' The assumption is that insights can be generated on demand and from analysis that can be done within minutes. Stephen's method, I thought, was a good way to help the business understand what they are asking of the analyst and how much effort it would take the data analyst to get this information. Then, finally, when do you need to know this? Some information is only useful during a certain window of time, and once that time window has passed the information no longer has the same impact or value. This usually occurs when the business needs certain analysis either to make a decision at a set deadline or send to an external party, for example providing numbers for public relations purposes or even investor relations purposes, where there is a publication deadline or where the sales or marketing team need some analysis for a pitch.

Figure 7.1   Value of data request

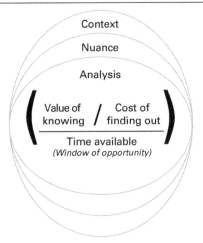

SOURCE Reproduced with permission of Stephen Kinsella, 2023

The way Stephen explained how he did this (see also Figure 7.1) was by asking the following questions:

- What is the value of knowing?
- What is the cost of finding out?
- What is the window for knowing this information?

This then provides the effort required to deliver the analysis. But he doesn't stop there, he explains that the analysis is influenced by several factors:

- the complexity of the analysis
- the nuance of the data
- the context of the business problem

When Stephen was describing this process, it made me realize that he was systemizing a process that all analysts probably have to make as a mental calculation before engaging in analysis. Those that do not, find that they either don't have enough time to do the analysis, or that the analysis that they could do in the time provided does not deliver the value that is needed by the business. Therefore, going back to the point of the attributes that data analysts and the team as a whole need to have is to be a partner to the business, asking the right questions and understanding why they want the analysis.

This shows the business that, through the actions of the data analysts, there is a nurturing of a data culture which values the outputs of the analysis. Another practice that over the years I have engaged with the different organizations is to instigate a cadence of delivering outputs which are highly visible in the organization. I also found that this practice has some longevity even after the data leader or most of the data team move on. This involves setting up regular reports to go out daily, weekly, monthly or quarterly, and these happen without fail so they are expected by the business and are highly visible reminders of the data team's outputs.

An absolute tragedy of a successful implementation of a data culture is when the culture is dependent on either the data leader or a handful of data analysts within the organization who are the lubricant to maintaining a healthy data culture. When they leave, the data culture in the organization dies or dissolves. This is where you need to build institutional wisdom, which is knowledge that resides within the organization long after those who have generated that knowledge have gone.

For example, after years of doing tests, a business learns that asking people to provide their name when signing up for a newsletter reduces signup, compared to when only an email is asked for. This knowledge should be passed on within the organization, mainly to the CRM team, and become wisdom. So when a new person joins and is being onboarded, the fact that this company doesn't ask for a name when asking for email signups should be automatically volunteered by the team to the new recruit, as part of why they do what they do. Or if someone from another team makes this suggestion, then rather than entertain this idea and go through the learning process that it doesn't work, everyone in the CRM team knows this as part of the team's wisdom. Obviously, this doesn't mean that you shouldn't retry things if you have evidence that customers will give their name. It just means that you don't repeat mistakes from the past when you have knowledge and wisdom within the team that can answer this question, without having to either run an analysis or run the test again. The existing members of the CRM team should be able to recall that the reason they don't ask for a name on email signup is because signup rates decrease by X per cent.

However, often the case is that no thought has been given to how knowledge and wisdom will be retained after the people who instigated and played a key role in creating this knowledge and wisdom have left the organization.

This is more common than it seems, and you will see companies rebooting their data strategy, hiring new people or teams to recreate a data culture. So a strategy I have implemented to avoid such an outcome is to set up a process of regular reporting, insights and storytelling. The implementation of this requires ownership of these outputs to be co-owned between the data team and other teams, with their contribution being part of the output and occasionally where possible delegating ownership of the outcome to the other teams.

Figure 7.2   Reporting cadence

| Daily flash reports | Weekly performance reports | Monthly insight sessions | Quarterly business reviews | Annual planning workshops |

This introduces practices into an organization which can be continued even after the people, mainly the data leader or data analysts who implemented the practices, have moved on.

The practices that I introduced were a series of regular reports or presentations, and consisted of daily (flash) reports that I mentioned previously, which play a strong role in building data intuition in analysts and help them become seen as experts, weekly performance report, monthly insight presentations, quarterly business reviews and annual planning workshops (Figure 7.2).

The order in which these are done does not need to start with flash reports and end with the annual planning workshops, and any one of them can be implemented at any time. At ITV, we started with the weekly performance report. This report was generated on Monday and contained data on the past week's performance of itv.com and ITV Player. Over time we introduced TV metrics from BARB, the TV audience measurement system used to measure TV viewership, but all these reports needed to be highly focused on the performance of the part of the business for which we were delivering. At Coca Cola, we delivered a weekly performance report for social media channels only for the global team. Our focus for that was the core KPIs for each social media channel and for a handful of countries that the global team were interested in. When an individual market wanted more metrics or KPIs included, we did not aim to add it to the current global weekly report but would recommend we create a separate one for them. Therefore, the weekly performance reports should focus on the core of what the business wants.

In other companies, I have suggested starting with a monthly insights presentation. My latest experience of doing this was for an organization that was very good at tactical reporting and the data team were exceptionally proficient at delivering numbers back to the business. However, there was no forum for them to discuss with a broader perspective where to focus efforts and what the data was telling them. This organization was a marketplace for independent sellers to sell branded content, and their tactical reporting was focused on bringing in new sellers and getting them to sell and promote their products. They knew from the data that the more sellers did this, the more they sold. However, if they took a step back, which is what these monthly insights presentations were showing them, then they could see that even though they were increasing the activity of sellers, this also resulted in more buyers coming to the site. However, the conversion rate for buyers was very low and if they focused their attention on improving the conversion rate of buyers, even by a few percentage points, they would see around a twenty to twenty-five per cent increase in sales.

At ITV, the weekly performance reports were introduced as one of the early practices to instil a data culture at ITV and make ITV Broadband, a subdivision where itv.com and ITV Player resided, more data-driven. Once we had established this practice, it became an expectation by the business to always receive this by midday Monday and it was used in operational planning. The business then even introduced an operational meeting first thing on Tuesday, which used this report as its basis to plan for the week.

The next thing to introduce was daily flash reports. For us this was relatively straightforward because, at that time, all our performance for itv.com and ITV Player were tracked by Omniture, now Adobe Analytics. I tasked my analysts to go across the business and identify the two or three core metrics each team or even individuals needed to understand how well they were doing their job and then we set up automated reports from Omniture to be sent to them first thing each morning. I also encouraged my data analysts to subscribe to these daily flash reports so they could build their knowledge of how the business performs and develop their data intuition.

Over time, these became critical components of how the business operated. I also have done the same at other organizations where I worked or consulted for. The weekly performance reports were the ones that became a staple deliverable that everyone valued and wanted. At ITV, even though people were using these reports, and even when I saw that the directors of ITV Broadband were printing these reports out and carrying them around with them so they could reference the numbers in meetings, I felt that a healthy data culture was only just developing but it needed something more. It was also the case that people within the business would be able to recall some key facts, which we reinforced through the weekly reports. However, I didn't feel that the data team was getting any feedback on the data, and we were just broadcasting the numbers in the form of daily and weekly reports, but the organization was not developing institutional wisdom. This is when, working with my manager, the MD of ITV Broadband, we came up with the idea of a monthly presentation where in collaboration with the different teams (sales, marketing, content, CRM, social media, technology and strategy), we would present back some KPIs and then delve deeper to provide some insights.

Having convinced my manager to sign off on a modest budget, I decided that the best time to do the monthly insight presentation would be on the second Friday of each month and start at 8.30am, offering attendees breakfast as an incentive to attend. That clearly worked. Over time, this monthly insight presentation became known as 'Breakfast with Shorful', which, though flattering and great for the ego, was not the way to instil a healthy data culture. Therefore, each invite emphasized it was the Online Insights Session, and those who came later into the organization and didn't know that I had set it up would eventually refer to it as the Online Monthly Insight Session.

The reason I settled on the second Friday of each month was so that it gave the team enough time to collate the data and develop the insights in collaboration with the different teams. The presentation itself lasted one and a half hours, and one of the dangers we found was that we tried to cram too much into each session. Over time, we learnt that when something big happened in the previous month or months, we would focus on that event rather than cover everything. So, the session eventually formed to have core KPIs presented upfront with different teams providing insights into why the numbers were what they were, and we then focused on a couple of areas of the business each month.

We booked the ITV boardroom to deliver this presentation, and each month the room was filled to capacity, with some standing (we hoped they all came along for the presentation and not just the breakfast). Eventually, this became a consistent pattern, and the team felt a sense of truly changing people's attitudes towards data and helping them to be more data-driven. At ITV we never did implement a quarterly business review. However, we contributed to others' quarterly planning outputs, such as investor relations who would consult us each quarter to obtain the relevant KPIs, and the rights reporting team who needed the numbers of video views in order to pay rights holders. We also did not instigate an annual planning session, but did create data and insights to assist with the annual planning for the business, which was run by the business executive for ITV broadband and the corporate strategy people.

In other places where I have instigated all of these elements, the reality is that some of these things work better than others. Elements of these practices continued even after I had moved on. However, when I speak with other data leaders about the regular cadence of reporting, insights and storytelling, they all mentioned that these set the foundation for a strong data culture as they are a very visible data output led by the data team.

At a recent social event with ex-colleagues from ITV I heard that the monthly insights sessions still continue, demonstrating that detaching these activities from individuals and teams and socializing them as organizational activities ensures their longevity and nurtures a positive data culture.

References

Ajzen, I (1991) The theory of planned behavior, *Organizational Behavior and Human Decision Processes*, 50(2), 179–211

Brookes, E (2023) The theory of planned behavior: Behavioral intention, Simply Psychology. www.simplypsychology.org/theory-of-planned-behavior.html (archived at https://perma.cc/3A6W-3HN6)

Kahneman, D (2011) *Thinking, Fast and Slow*, Farrar, Straus and Giroux, New York

Skinner, B F (1948) 'Superstition' in the pigeon, *Journal of Experimental Psychology*, 38(2), 168–72

When you know you have a healthy data culture 8

Building the right stakeholder relationships and how to evolve the team

In organizations that do not have a healthy data culture, I have observed leadership arguing or debating over a decision and not even considering referring to any data or analysis to settle the debate. In healthy data culture, what I have seen is that when individuals in an organization need to make a decision, especially one that requires a change that could impact revenue or some other success measure, they will ask for data on past changes. Even before the meeting where the decision will be made, requests would have been made to the data team for analysis that could help inform their decision.

Where no such data exists, they would consult the data team on how they could get this data and would propose ideas such as A/B testing. Consulting the data team and asking for ways to quantify the impact of changes, either through data analysis or experimentation, would not be ideas or concepts that the business needs to be convinced of – it will form part of the organizational process when making key decisions. Even after having all this information, I have seen organizations make decisions that are not supported by the facts. I always tell my team that this is OK. Not all decisions have to be based on data, as long as the business leaders have the information to hand. Even if they don't use it, and they can make a compelling case on why they are not using it, then as leaders of the business they are entitled to make that decision. The data team can only advise and recommend ways forward. The actual decision lies with those empowered to make it.

In the past, I consulted for a very large publisher who wanted to create a new offering aligned to their main publication. The new publication or supplement was seeking to do something different to what they normally did. My team was asked to analyse the current data and provide recommendations on how best to launch this new supplement. Now, the business already had other different supplements connected to the main publication, but these were essentially the same as the main publication but focused on a particular theme or topic area. This new supplement was being launched mainly as a lead generation mechanism for their subscription and event businesses. The majority of the content was written by guest writers and sat behind a registration wall, meaning visitors had to create a free account, giving their name and email to view the content.

Even though the analysis showed that a small but sizeable portion of visitors did visit the existing supplements, these were free to view, and the engagement was as high as the main publication. What we didn't have data on was what would happen if visitors were asked to register. We ran some scenarios based on industry conversion numbers, and tried to forecast how many visitors and leads this new subsection would get. What we discovered was not very convincing. Using industry conversion rates and the forecasted volumes of visitors to this new supplement, the numbers would be too low for the supplement to be profitable. As a lead generation mechanism, we modelled how many visitors they could convert to subscribers or attend their events, and again the evidence was not that great. No matter how we looked at the data, we couldn't find a scenario where it would support putting a registration wall before the content on this subsection and we didn't want to stretch the modelling too far that it just became fiction.

After we presented the findings to the business, they acknowledged that, based on the available evidence, it didn't seem like there was support for this new supplement. However, they wanted to continue with it. Firstly, they believed that, as the content would be written by prominent guest writers, they would get more interest in that supplement than other supplements they have previously launched. Secondly, they also acknowledged that they just didn't know how successful it would be and the investment in this supplement as a learning experience was justified, as they needed to increase their lead generation activity as subscriptions and attendances at events were declining.

This showed an organization that was very mature in its journey to be data-driven and had developed a healthy data culture where they acknowledged what the data was telling them, but they felt able to justify why they made the decisions owing to the data and not in spite of it.

In this case, the leadership team agreed that, even though this was a big investment, they would be closely monitoring the data to check in on performance and conversion rates for leads and make adjustments to the supplement as needed. Incidentally, this organization had their own data team, and it was their CDO who brought us in. This is another sign of a healthy data culture where the existing team realize their limitations, both in terms of capacity and skills, and are willing to bring in help without feeling threatened. The data team, from what I could see, were positively contributing to our work, and saw this as a collective effort.

A dysfunctional data culture would not have functioned in that way. One thing that stands out when a data culture is not working is the amount of rivalry or friction between teams. A lack of cross-functional collaboration points to an organization that hasn't aligned on core and common measures of success. Where teams from different functions collaborate, it's automatic for them to include someone from the data team in the decision-making process, or at a minimum go armed with data and analysis, to support or dispute a position. Whenever I work with a company, especially on a novel problem, I can judge the health or strength of the data culture by who they invite to the initial meeting with me. If there is no one from the data team or who is managing or leading a data function, then it becomes clear that there is a lack of value attached to the data team and to the data. Often these organizations will bring me and my consultancy in to do something that the existing data team have said is not possible or difficult with the current data and infrastructure.

After some investigation, more often than not, what the data team has said is usually true and then we are asked to propose an alternative solution. Again, this is something that the data team could do, but for whatever reason the organization does not value the opinions or contributions of the data team. This can lead occasionally to a bad or toxic data culture. When speaking with Adam Wright, he said that when you end up in this situation you can see behavioural issues in the data team, from continuous complaining about the business, to not attending meetings or, when attending, being confrontational or disengaged.

The business then reacts to this by claiming all problems in how the company is performing are because they do not have the right data or that they can't trust the data. Eventually, the business starts to challenge every piece of analysis or ignore it, without even making an effort to engage with the data team to fix it. The opposite of that is when you see the values of data transcend beyond the data team who champion it. When you have a healthy data culture, it is easy to identify and empower data champions within the organization and these individuals then serve as advocates for data usage. They may even become promoters of data, helping others understand and realize its benefits. You even end up in situations where individuals within the organization who are not part of the data team actively propose and contribute to data-related initiatives. As an outside observer, this always demonstrates to me that the data culture is ingrained at all levels. It's one of the things I discussed with Julie Screech. When you build a healthy data culture, data then just becomes something the business does without being aware that they are doing it. It almost becomes automatic and intuitive, and the organization just uses data without it seeming like an add on or bolt on.

This means that since use of data is mainstream, the access to data is seamless, without any major obstacles for anyone in the organization who wants to retrieve and analyse the data. A good indicator of that in an organization is if someone new asks for a number, a report or piece of analysis, the effort to get this is minimal and either the person asked can get it, or they instinctively know who in the data team or group of individuals they should ask to get the data. They are also confident they will get something back that answers the question.

The other thing you will notice is that, even with ease of access to data, the organization takes data privacy and protection seriously, ensuring that when returning data, even if it is to internal stakeholders, they make sure no data is presented that doesn't need to be there, including stripping away any personally identifiable information, or commercially sensitive information. The institutional wisdom around data is transmitted through daily practices so that anyone new to the organization, through observation, knows what good looks like.

Evolution of stakeholder relationships

In a data-driven organization, stakeholder relationships evolve to become more informed, collaborative and focused on data-driven insights. With data informing most decisions, stakeholders from different departments collaborate more closely owing to having access to data-driven insights. They recognize the value of cross-functional cooperation to address complex challenges. An organization that has a healthy data culture is one where all parts of the business see every problem as their problem. Using data to have a common dialogue, they can identify how their efforts can contribute to solving the problem.

This is because data-driven insights empower stakeholders to make more informed decisions and measure performance. Decisions are backed by data, reducing reliance on gut feelings or assumptions. When you have this common understanding, you as an organization have shared goals and objectives, and decisions made are based on a common understanding of the truth based on data. For the data team, this translates into being facilitators of decision-making and no longer having to continually be a champion or advocate of data.

As a data leader, what you will notice when a healthy data culture takes hold is that your engagement and relationship with stakeholders changes. Instead of trying to get time in their diary to convince and encourage them to use data, you will find that your stakeholders will seek you or your team out. When you are proactively invited to kick off meetings or even asked to join directors at senior leadership meetings that you had not previously been invited to, then the dynamics between the data team and the rest of the organization have changed. As one client put it to me, 'We see our data team as partners and advisers – they are not seen as "nice to have", a service or back-office function that is seen as a cost centre, but rather as a critical part of the organization.'

As a data leader, you will notice that you start moving away from simply working on the data and the analysis done in the organization and that you are drawn into more strategic and planning meetings, helping the business understand how they can use data and what it means. This will typically creep up on you slowly, and you may notice that you are no longer checking in with your team as often as you used to. As mentioned in Chapter 6, being needed is a great position to be in, for you and your team. However, it is then easy for egos to start surfacing, and therefore it's important that you understand this and mentor your team to remain trusted advisers to the business, and not to fall into the traps mentioned in Chapter 5.

Another common problem or challenge is that you find that you are cancelling one-to-one sessions with your senior team or analyst, and leaving them to get on with the work, whilst you integrate yourself more with other parts of the business's decision-making process. This is why it is important to make sure you hire the right people for the time. At this stage, having a rock-star analyst can prove challenging, if not dangerous, to the data culture you and the team have created. Not being close to what they are doing means that, owing to their nature, they will independently decide what they do, and this may not align with what is expected of them.

When I was at Wunderman (as of writing this book in late 2023, they are now VML), I inherited a very small team of around 8 to 10 data analysts. Over my tenure, I grew that team to over 60 in the London office, and another 60 to 70 in offshore offices. In the beginning I was very much involved in the day-to-day activity, I knew what the team was working on, and I even had the luxury to get involved in some of the analysis. However, as the team grew, I found that my diary became more and more packed, and I was attending meetings which were more about looking forward and planning than about what was needed by clients now. This meant that I was not close to the work being done, and if I was in a meeting with a client or partner, and something was raised about the work, I was not in a position to comment on it as I didn't have full visibility on the detail of the work. However, I had created a small leadership team who reported to me and I trusted them to manage the work.

This is something you need to become comfortable with, as a data leader. You need to get accustomed to not being as close to the detail of delivery. Your relationship with stakeholders has changed, and so have the dynamics between your team and the organization. Hopefully, you have built a team you trust and that trust is shared by the organization, which means that they can approach the data team directly and expect the same level and quality of service as they would if they approached you directly.

Unfortunately, this is not something that is always universal across the organization. In some roles, I had built up a team and I believed they were at a level where they could operate without needing me to be involved in the granular day-to-day activities. As a data leader, you find, as mentioned above, a requirement to detach yourself from the detail of what is going on, for one reason or another. You will know when the right moment is when you have a team who you trust to deliver without your oversight. In this one organization, as the team grew and when I thought we had the beginnings of a healthy data culture emerging, I left many of the day-to-day activities to be wholly managed by the team between them.

However, the trust I had in my team was not reflected by all of my senior stakeholders, and one in particular felt that they were not getting what they needed from the data team. This was a combination of them being new, having poorly defined requirements and expectations, and not fully understanding the remit of the data team. It also didn't help that the data team didn't take the time to understand what this stakeholder was conveying and made too many assumptions based on previous interactions with other stakeholders. This led to a series of poor interactions between this individual and the team, and soon enough it was escalated to me.

The issue was that this new person didn't have any of the context of why the organization operated the way it did, and the team they joined, the account management team, typically did not have a good understanding of the work of the data team. It was one of the teams in the organization that I spent a considerable amount of time with, to help them understand how the data team worked, the value of our work and how it could empower and help them in their role. In my experience, account management teams at agencies sometimes see data teams as a support function for them. This new person held this view. As my team engaged with them as partners, this new person felt that they were not just getting the outputs they needed, but were faced with data analysts who probed, quizzed and challenged the reason for the request.

I should have coached the team to engage differently with someone who was new to the organization, and especially conveyed my knowledge of working with account management and the challenges I had faced. This would have allowed the data analysts to adapt their style for when new people joined and work with them so that they became socialized to the way the organization used data and engaged with the data team. What this episode highlighted is that you can't prematurely expect things to work just because you have the beginnings of a healthy data culture. You need to continually adapt and evolve the practices of the data team, so that they can account for most eventualities.

One of those aspects is a mutual understanding between the data team and the stakeholders. In the example above, my team assumed that all stakeholders held the same understanding of data and it didn't occur to them that someone new would need to be socialized into our ways of working. The new staff member may also have come from an organization with a different data culture. Therefore, in the early days in building a data culture, we should have allowed for that.

The mistake I made was not proactively having an introductory meeting with this person and explaining how the data team operated and what our values, vision and goals were. This opportunity would have also allowed the person to share their perspectives on the use of data, and the practices that may have been prominent in their previous organization. One of the data leaders I spoke to when writing this book said that he would always hold two introductory meetings with new employees. The first meeting was for the new employee to just complain about all the issues they have with data, and the data team. The second was to understand what they wanted to achieve. He said that by giving them a complaining session, he could then assess what their expectations were and use that knowledge when having the second meeting about what they wanted to achieve, and address or challenge their expectations.

This episode with the account management leader demonstrated to the team that we probably didn't have a strong data culture yet, even though we felt that we had made so much progress, and in our discussions on how to mitigate this in the future, the team suggested that they proactively become part of a 'new joiners' induction process and use early engagements with the new joiner to demonstrate and showcase how they work with the rest of the organization. A healthier data culture would have had the account management team manifesting good data practices. This would then have been evident to the new person, who would then have understood that data and the data team were used differently than in their previous organization.

Evolving the team

In Chapter 6 I referred to the trusted lieutenant, someone every data leader should seek to find amongst their team. This person becomes more important as a data culture embeds itself in an organization. Like any culture, it's not a final end point or a static phenomenon. It changes, it evolves, and it reacts to the agents which create, influence and contribute to that culture.

As a data leader you need to be aware of that. A consequence of an organization developing a data culture and wanting to be data-driven is that as a data leader you become drawn into more decision-making engagements, typically meaning your diary is filled with attending meetings and writing presentations. Therefore, you become more detached from the actual activities of the team. Part of that is understanding the evolving needs of stakeholders and the organization.

You therefore need your team to evolve to become receptors of how the organization is changing, and they must be coached, mentored and empowered to adapt or have the opportunity to consult you about how to react to these changes. When you are busy, it's tempting to delegate everything and then become too detached, so that you don't become aware of issues which could build up and often shatter the progress the organization has made in being data-driven.

I've seen too often small issues build up and then the cumulative effect shatters or sets back the progress the organization has made in developing a data culture. To counter this, you need someone who will be your eyes and ears. They need to also be someone who you feel is worth investing in, so you can delegate responsibilities and authority.

My philosophy has always been that when I find my trusted lieutenant I should be willing to invest my time and effort so that one day they can replace me. That should be the objective of all good data leaders. Once you have that mindset, you can then break free from the trap of everyone relying on you to get things done. It's one of the ways the data team needs to evolve. It shows the basis of a healthy data culture. The data team needs to be flatter, and less hierarchical, which means that more of the individuals in the data team need to take on a more visible role across the organization. As mentioned in the previous chapter, a way to develop a data culture is by instigating behaviours and practices by the data team, which others can then mimic. One way to make this sustainable is to allow individuals in the data team to take ownership and then ultimately become responsible for the data culture.

At ITV, for example, the monthly presentation was eventually handed over to one of my senior analysts. This presentation would then have very little input from me. It didn't mean I was totally detached from the creation of the presentation, but the final state was the team creating the presentation and a couple of days before the presentation session the team would do a rehearsal presentation with me, and I as well as others would provide our feedback.

When you have established a healthy data culture, you will witness members of your data team taking ownership of different activities with hardly any input from you. So, this goes back to the trusted lieutenant. You need someone who can get on with running the team, managing the workload and dealing with stakeholders. Depending on the size of the data team, you may have more than one, and they may be responsible for different areas. But they will all feel empowered to act autonomously because in an organization with a healthy data culture they will know how to behave and act. Even beyond the trusted lieutenant, others in the data team should know how to behave, as observation of good practices should be widespread so even new data analysts can pick it up by just watching what others do.

It's important to stress here that one of the ways this happens is if there are initially shared values between the data leader and their team, and those shared values are agreed across the organization. Without these shared values of how and when to use data and what being data-driven means, it's hard for the rest of the data team to know what good looks like or what you want the team to achieve. For these values to be shared, as a data leader, instead of just speaking about them, you need to start demonstrating tangibly what good looks like. This can take the form of presenting what success looks like, educating others on data best practices, and reflecting these values in your work.

If your team observes you behaving contrary to the values you speak of, then it easily erodes the positive team dynamics. One of the values I speak of in terms of being data-driven is not showing bias when doing any analysis. As mentioned in Chapter 5, being biased, even if it is with good intentions, creates silos and isolates the data team. I'm therefore extremely cautious when presenting any work my team has done that could be perceived as supporting a particular viewpoint. I ask my team always to present findings that genuinely support a viewpoint with an element of objectivity and consideration. Being enthusiastic is great when a result supports a hypothesis, but be mindful that others may have competing views, and in supporting one view you may be alienating another.

In the early days, this may not be so much of an issue as you try to accumulate small wins, but later, when a data culture has established itself in the organization, the value of what the data team presents increases in status. As a data leader you need to be aware of this, as it's easy to be thought of as taking sides as there is more at stake when an organization takes data seriously.

As an example, I worked with a very large telecommunications company looking at customer lifetime value (LTV). Of the many hypotheses they had about increasing lifetime value, two dominated. One was to focus on existing high-value customers and increase their value. The other was to focus on low-value customers and commit efforts and budget to retain them. Both of these were valid, and the analysis did suggest that, at a customer level, increasing the lifetime value of high-value customers would result in more average revenue per user (ARPU) than focusing on low-value customers. However, if efforts were made to retain low-value customers, then even though their lifetime value was lower than high-value customers, there were significantly more of them, and as a cohort or group they generated more total revenue.

So, when presenting the analysis my team did, we presented both viewpoints, and concluded that as this project was looking at LTV and ARPU, then growing high-value customers was a better approach than low-value customers. However, we did point out that focusing on low-value customers, in terms of retention, would not substantially increase LTV and ARPU, but would generate more total revenue. This positioned the data team as a neutral player in this decision-making process, and only when they asked for my opinion did I express my view that, as a business, if you are looking for total growth then the better ROI would come from retaining low-value customers than trying to further grow high-value customers.

This episode also demonstrated to my team that, even though we do not show bias when doing analysis, we are entitled to our viewpoint and organizations will typically seek out those with data expertise for their insights and recommendations. By doing this, as a data leader you will become a key contributor to strategic discussions, as should your team, as the data culture matures.

A healthy data culture isn't a fixed state. How healthy or unhealthy it is will depend on how the team evolves. Part of that is how the data team evolves its relationship with the rest of the organization. The ability to listen to feedback and adapt as your organization evolves is key to sustaining a healthy data culture. Being inflexible in your approach as a data leader can lead to all your hard work being undermined.

How to maintain and measure a data culture

9

How do you know when you have succeeded?

You would think that a book on data culture would advocate having many KPIs to measure how a data culture is developing in your organization. However, even though you can set KPIs to measure behaviours and practices, you can only infer the intention behind the behaviours and the data culture that exists. When measuring the success of anything, I am an advocate for having robust KPIs that can be analysed to evaluate how things are going. If you are launching a CRM programme, you need to have KPIs to determine whether it has been successful and leads to an increase in customer value. If you are introducing a paywall subscription service for an ad-funded publication, does the revenue from subscription exceed the revenue from ads for subscribers?

However, beyond the KPIs you also need to have qualitative measures that allow you to understand the 'why'. For example, people may be willing to put up with a lot of barriers to access the content or services they need or want, especially if that content or services are free. However, qualitatively they may be unsatisfied or even angry with the user experience. Just observing the quantitative KPIs would show that people are doing what you want them to do, but they may not be happy doing it.

Measuring a healthy data culture

With data culture, just observing the behaviour is not enough. The intention should also be the desire to be a data-driven organization. Defining a healthy data culture is often hard in terms of quantification and, like all cultures, it is often what is observed as the norm that defines the status of a culture. The data leaders I interviewed for this book suggested a number of ways to understand the state of your data culture:

- Is there a person from the data team in every meeting? Is the voice of data heard in those forums?
- Does the business have a sensible number of KPIs which they refer to in order to make decisions?
- Does the business care about data? Do C-suite leaders use the dashboards? Does the CEO value these dashboards without always questioning their value?
- Does the business use data from a single source of truth and point to it when evaluating performance?
- Does the business stay consistent in its use of data and not use third-party data to make a point and contradict internal data?
- Is the organization confident in the data and its accuracy?
- Is the language used around data positive, where benefits are mentioned more than challenges?
- Is the data team seen as a benefit to the organization and not always referred to as a cost centre?

Again, this starts at the top, so as a data leader you need to continuously ensure that top leadership remains committed to the data culture. Leadership should consistently promote data-driven practices and set an example. I'm not sure you can set a KPI or measure this behaviour systematically, but it should be observable in your organization. Senior leaders should more often than not be data-driven in their regular decision-making and more so when it comes to the most critical decisions.

Beyond referring to data for decision-making, they should also encourage data-driven projects, and proactively promote the initiation of data-driven projects that showcase the value of the organization's data culture. For example, where a new reporting or data visualization solution is being deployed, or a new predictive model is being built, senior leaders should acknowledge their development and speak of the benefits they will bring to the organization. The engagement with these projects helps sustain enthusiasm and momentum as they show the rest of the business that the leadership is still engaged with data. Another observable behaviour should be the celebration and recognition of teams and individuals who achieve significant outcomes through data-driven initiatives. Public recognition reinforces the importance of a healthy data culture. This should occur often enough that people can very easily recall the last time the data team was recognized. As a data leader, it is worth using these instances of being recognized to baseline the significance of data in the organization and encourage senior leadership about the importance of recognizing the data team for their work when interest in data may be waning.

However, a word of caution is also needed. I have seen too many instances of senior leadership talking about and promoting data-related initiatives in their organization. Every other presentation they do mentions the use of data. However, there is no genuine intention to be data-driven. From an observable metric of senior leadership encouraging and promoting data initiatives this seems to be happening, but in reality there may not be the actions to back up those mentions and the organization does not move forward with being data-driven. These should be followed up with resources and budget to realize these initiatives. As a data leader, you will note how often words turn into action and set a benchmark for how seriously the senior leadership, and therefore the organization, has established a data culture.

There should also be a general consensus in the organization that data is embedded in processes. What this should look like is that data is integrated into existing business processes and decision-making practices. This ensures that data is consistently considered in day-to-day operations. The way to measure this is twofold, and usually involves the inverse of what a healthy data culture should look like, in other words what a poor data culture looks like. The first way is to quantify how many decisions are made without using data. This will become obvious once the decision has been executed and the question of how it performed arises. In my experience this is typically when the data team first hears about it. The other is when the data team is an afterthought and is either invited to the meeting at the last minute or consulted after the decision-making meeting and prior to finalizing a decision. (I've even had several cases where I was asked by senior leadership to join a meeting as it was happening, as they had forgotten to invite someone from data.) It's worth in your personal development reviews with your manager to try to quantify how often this happens. If it's only once or twice a year then the organization can be forgiven, but if it happens relatively frequently it suggests a healthy and strong data culture is not present in the organization.

You could also make this systematic by formally and informally collecting feedback from all employees in an organization of their experience of using and interacting with data initiatives. I tried to do this at one agency, which include periodically doing a live survey during some of the company's monthly updates. What is difficult is getting the balance right between people complaining about not getting the data they need and constructive feedback that allows you to assess the strength of the data culture. However, what these surveys did highlight was the improvement in data literacy within this organization, and the use of agreed and correct terms increasing over time, which suggested that a data culture was maturing. I've also monitored how many employees in the organization, outside the data team, attend data-related training and workshops. A good example is when a marketing or advertising technology is procured. These will often have an analytics module. It is quite telling of a healthy data culture to see how many non-data people complete this training.

In one company I consulted for, I witnessed behaviours which suggested there was a healthy data culture. The data team had developed a series of models that increased the basket size and average revenue per user on their ecommerce platform. What this meant was that the data initiatives were delivering very tangible benefits, and the organization was invested in making sure they performed. This led to meetings where the performance of the models was discussed. Even without the data team needing to be present, it seemed most people had access to the performance measures for this model. There was also frequent discussion about what other data initiatives could be suggested to the data team, and how they could measure success. It was a pleasure to see mature data literacy present in the organization, with a healthy debate around what success would look like and agreeing on success measures.

Seeing how the data team was involved and the collaboration between the different departments in ensuring that data initiatives were successfully implemented was a clear sign of a healthy data culture. Working across this organization, another measure of a healthy data culture was the use of data by most employees in the organization when backing up their ideas. I was very much impressed when I sat in a CRM team meeting at this organization, where the starting point of the meeting was reviewing the performance of past email campaigns, and using that as the basis of future campaigns. What this suggested was that the company had succeeded in establishing a healthy data culture. When ideas were being suggested, most of them had at least some data to back them up. The CRM team would discuss how they had asked for a piece of analysis after they had an idea for a new campaign and how that data supported the idea they were proposing. There was no need for a data analyst to be present at this meeting I attended and each person took ownership for using data.

Maintaining a healthy data culture

Sometime in the pursuit to measure what success looks like, we overlook how to maintain a data culture. A data culture does not have an end state and it will evolve as the organization evolves. This may mean that measures of success also need to change. Ideally, a data culture would be sustained organically within an organization, with each employee being an active agent who exhibits positive data practices. But, if this is not the case, and a data culture is maintained owing to the sheer effort of the data leader and data team, then when key members of the data team leave, cracks start to form in the data culture.

Therefore, maintaining a data culture and being able to measure its health requires a way to measure how the organization as a whole is being data-driven. I've always tried to create data champions within the organization, and the way to do this is to make data integral to their success. When I set up the CRM function at ITV and hired the first CRM manager, my ambition was for this function to be data-driven from the outset. We even went as far as calculating the revenue per user per email campaign. Over time, the CRM manager became a data champion, ensuring that data was collected robustly and was easily accessible. The intention may have been selfish to ensure they could demonstrate the success of their CRM activities, but the outcome was to create a data champion within the organization who promoted the use of data to demonstrate performance and success. In another organization, I engaged with key individuals who I believed would be good data champions. We worked together to integrate the way they demonstrated success by using data to calculate the return on investment for the work they did. I was able to ensure that the realm of data went beyond that of the data team and that data as an asset belonged to other teams as well.

Something that helps these teams or individuals advocate and champion data is to help them create benchmarks for what good looks like. Often, you can compare the performance of activities with past activities, but how do you know if what you are seeing is good? It is often difficult for other teams to say whether the results they are seeing for the work they are doing is good or bad, as they have no reference point. This makes them hesitant to champion the use of data. Helping establish benchmarks for what good looks like, the data team can empower others to become data champions, as they can use these benchmarks to demonstrate how they are performing. Benchmarks created by the data team, who are perceived as independent in a healthy data culture, make it easier for others to use data to demonstrate success and therefore champion it.

Again, as mentioned in several chapters, the data team needs to be unbiased and not take sides. To maintain a healthy data culture, it's important to keep an eye on this. A measure of this is to understand the number of teams who proactively ask for data representation in their decision-making practices. If it is the case that only a select few do all the time, and data representation is not sought out across the whole organization, then it would suggest that you are not maintaining a healthy data culture. Though it does stretch the data team, being asked to be involved across the business is a good measure of success.

Data culture is company culture

Of all the data leaders I spoke with, their ultimate measure of success in establishing a data culture is when they feel that data culture becomes just part of the overall company culture. Their ambition is that what they do becomes what everyone else in the organization eventually does. Data shouldn't be seen as the domain of a particular team. Even if that means that the data team or its responsibilities become dispersed throughout the organization, they believe that this is a good thing, as it shows they have succeeded. As Julie Screech put it, data can be seen as a river running through an organization, where each team takes buckets of water to do what they need.

In addition to seeing different teams use data as part of their daily practices, it is also about adopting wider data practices, such as innovation and experimentation. When different teams experiment with data and propose innovative solutions, such as developing new metrics or proposing new ways to collect data, it leads to continuous improvements and the maintenance of a healthy data culture. It ensures that the organization's data stays up to date and is always relevant.

At times this may mean that an organization needs to revisit how it measures success and have a healthy debate about change. This could range from gradually changing reports and dashboards to reflect what an organization considers important currently to updating predictive and prescriptive models to account for what it wants its customers to do next. A healthy data culture will allow the organization to engage in how it uses data without needing the data team to be part of every discussion. This evolution of the use of data, originating from the organization and typically outside of the data team, maintains a healthy data culture, and can serve as a useful measure of what good looks like when measuring data culture. It also serves as a feedback loop for the data leader to understand and keep a pulse on what is important for the business, how the business is changing its use of data and how they should evolve to reflect these changes. By maintaining a proactive approach to the use of data and consistently aligning your efforts with the organization's goals, you can ensure that the data culture remains vibrant, effective and aligned with the company's mission and values.

When I have worked with an organization to create a data strategy, my plans always have a continuous development loop at the end. When I am asked why I don't have an end point for the data strategy, I explain that a data strategy is there to guide the organization in creating a positive data culture. But, like all strategies, it needs to have the flexibility to evolve and change as internal and external factors influence and create change. In the fast-evolving data landscape, there are several factors that will impact how data strategies need to change.

One of these is the regulatory environment. As more and more regulation and legislation is introduced to protect consumers and their data, as a data leader you need to keep informed of these developments and help the company adapt. Even when major players in this space change their practices and technology, how a company adapts and evolves could have a major impact on its success. For example, I am working with several companies where the blocking of third-party cookies by the major browsers and mobile OS, like Apple, Google and Mozilla, is creating challenges in measuring the effectiveness of their digital marketing and advertising activities. For some it has forced them to look at how they measure digital marketing and for others it has caused them to explore different analytical methodologies. We have even gone as far as inventing new analytical techniques which combine the robustness of econometrics and the power of machine learning to help businesses overcome this challenge. These novel and innovative approaches are uncomfortable for any organization, but those with a healthy data culture find them much easier to embrace.

The success of a healthy data culture is evident through an organization's confidence in evolving how it accepts and adapts to change in the data landscape. A major upheaval will be presented by the integration of generative AI within organizational processes. How does an organization address the ethical issues that AI will present? If it has a regular forum to assess data ethics and compliance practices, this would serve as a measure of a healthy data culture. Another useful measure would be being able to quantify whether employees are following ethical guidelines in data usage. This one is essential to measure, not just to determine a healthy data culture but also to identify the risk posed to the organization if ethical guidelines in data usage are not adhered to. This may be something the data leader can measure through the information security compliance team, helping them to understand whether data is being used responsibly. This is especially critical when it comes to customer data which, if used inappropriately, can result in an organization receiving penalties including fines.

Data culture is not a goal. It is an ongoing ambition, and all organizations need to understand that maintaining one requires ongoing measurement. It is simply not the case that when certain KPIs have been achieved an organization is suddenly data-driven. As an ambition, it requires the organization to adapt and change as internal and external factors dictate and influence the organization's data culture. Being successful in creating a data culture means understanding that being data-driven is a journey, not a destination.

What you can achieve with a good data culture in your organization

10

A good data culture in an organization can bring about a wide range of benefits and positive outcomes. These go significantly beyond the obvious benefits of informed decision-making, being data-driven, developing data products, and being more experimental and innovative. Simply put, a strong data culture leads to more things being possible. Often this will translate into wider applications of data, which may include the commercialization of data, so that the data team become revenue generators. Abs Owdud mentions that in some companies like Quidco, where he worked, the data team generated revenue through the data products they created, such as recommendation engines. Other companies I have worked with have also assigned revenue to data products like cross-sell models. Where organizations can productize their data services, they can make data a revenue generation function instead of a cost centre.

Other aspects that can be achieved are things like operational efficiencies. Data helps identify inefficiencies, bottlenecks, and areas for improvement, leading to streamlined processes and cost savings. In addition, by having a good data culture, an organization can be far more effective in delivering change, have a better understand of what success looks like and become robust in measuring and working towards success. These tangible benefits lead to a company delivering projects and initiatives which drive growth and competitive advantage.

A happy team

Whilst writing this book, I consulted several data leaders and we all agreed that beyond these commercial successes there were cultural changes that a good data culture brings. These inevitably lead directly or indirectly to an organization's success. Fayez Shriwardhankar mentioned that when you have a good data culture you have a happy and relaxed team that is willing to ask questions and engage with the organization. They also take pride in their work and ultimately deliver work of high value to the business. He used a good analogy. The team should be like a swan – very calm on the surface, but busy working behind the scenes to make things happen.

Others such as Adam Wright discussed how having a good data culture meant that it was easier to retain the team, and even if there were some team members who did not align with the team's values and vision, it was much easier to deal with them if the overall data culture was strong. Going back to my discussion of the rock-star analysts in Chapter 6, in an organization with a good data culture, if you were to hire one of these rock-star analysts later in your data journey they would not be able to create as much disruption as if they were hired early. A good data culture will require them to be collaborative and open, demonstrating transparency and team work. If they did not do this, their behaviour would be seen as abnormal and it would be easier for you as a data leader to point out how they should work and behave.

If you do happen to have a rock-star analyst later in your data journey, it could become a source of tension in the team, as you have built a data function that is collaborative and aligned. Someone who wishes to operate independently and with little transparency would not fit in. Delaying the decision to deal with them can result in more problems, and in my experience unsettle the other members of the team. Having a healthy data culture means that you can address their behaviours, actions and practices constructively and within the framework of what is expected of everyone. Should they not wish to align with these values, vision and practices, then my advice has always been to help them move on. Keeping them in the long term doesn't work out and they end up not only destabilizing the team, but also setting back the development of the data culture.

When it comes to recruiting, a good data culture makes it easier to hire. A good data culture becomes one of the reasons why data professionals want to join your organization. When an organization celebrates success, it becomes much easier to celebrate these successes publicly, through posts on social media, through PR or even through entering awards. This makes it easier to promote your healthy data culture and encourage new data analysts to join your team. I have found that organizations that promote their data successes frequently foster a healthy data culture which makes recruiting data analysts much easier.

Prospective analysts will hear about 'hero' case studies where the team has built something that has delivered significant revenue or value for the business. The value attached to the data team increases and its activities become more well-known. If the organization is known to always be optimizing with data, trying to get just one per cent better after each initiative, or using data for continuous improvement, then prospective analysts will want to work at such an organization that attaches importance to data.

Another aspect of a healthy data culture that impacts team dynamics is that the team are more confident in their work and don't always feel like they have to prove their value. As Stephen Kinsella mentioned, when an organization has a healthy data culture it is easier for the data leader to delegate more to the rest of the data team. The team becomes more proactive and also hears more often about what the organization wants to achieve. Both Stephen and Fayez mentioned that the team will find that the organization is more willing to listen as you now have their attention. They also discussed that it is also easier for the team to have access to the right forums, with their voices being heard and decisions being trusted. This leads to the team making better decisions and delivering better outputs, which in turn leads to more trust. This then leads to the team delivering even better results. The business will also proactively seek the counsel of the data team, and see them as advisers.

Something else that Lara Izlan mentions was that the business starts to play back the benefits of data by explaining and showcasing how data has helped with a decision or shown the success of an initiative, without the need for any prompting from the data leader or data team. This only becomes possible when a healthy data culture has taken hold, as it becomes part of what the organization does well. Min Bhogaita also mentions that when a healthy data culture takes hold in an organization, it is much easier to convince the business to run pilots. Lara echoes this point by saying that when this happens, the organization starts to engage with experimentation and self-service of analytics. The business is also then likely to acquire the right data tools to achieve its goals.

With a happier data team, and the ability to more easily attract and retain data analysts, a good data culture allows the business to have some stability in the team. This means that they can derive more benefit from data than the obvious avenues, such as just reporting or statistical models. For example, an ecommerce company I worked with wanted to explore how the data they collected about what customers purchased, browsed and searched for could be used to create partnerships with other companies. The data team had got them to a place where they had good data they could trust, the systems in place to easily access and run reports for decision-making, and an infrastructure that allowed them to run predictive and prescriptive models on the ecommerce platform.

A more ambitious organization

However, the senior leadership had become more ambitious because of the value they were seeing being demonstrated by the data team and the wider organization. They wanted to see if the data they collected, stored and processed could be used to further drive, and potentially direct, revenue. What they wanted to understand was whether the data they held had value to partner companies or other third parties. Having looked at their data, I suggested many avenues of value they could explore, ranging from feeding insights back to merchandisers about demand and interest in their products, to using the search on their ecommerce platform to understand how customers were finding their products and potentially having variable pricing based on search demand, to working with research agencies to deliver market and industry insights. We even went as far as trying to quantify the value of the data they held as if it were a business asset. With the development of a healthy data culture, the organization and especially the senior leadership had begun to see data as an asset, one to be leveraged and commercialized and not just something that they needed to invest in to stay relevant and competitive.

This shift in mindset is quite common when an organization develops a good data culture. A value mindset about data is formed, moving away from seeing data as a cost centre to an asset or revenue generator. Companies start to see how they can move beyond the direct benefits of data to a wider set of benefits. It is not uncommon for organizations to derive financial gain from the data they collect, by commercializing the insights or opportunities it may present. This, however, is done by adopting ethical guidelines so that data is not misused or 'sold' to third parties, which would breach the agreement they have with their customers. Instead, companies are looking at ways in which aggregate data, or insights derived from the data, can help them stay competitive and also allow them to make data a revenue-driving asset.

Most companies might not succeed in doing this. When I've explored these ideas with a variety of companies, either they do not have the right data for commercial exploitation or the data they do have poses too much of a significant risk to be exposed externally. However, it is encouraging to see companies willing to explore and experiment. Obviously, some will try to do this without having first developed a healthy data culture, and it is those who will abuse the trust given to them by customers when collecting and using their data. Often this will occur with consequences that are quite public and damaging to the reputation of the company.

A good data culture often results in the organization being very strategically aligned, and this ensures that data initiatives are aligned with the organization's goals and priorities. They are more aware of the potential risks of using data and are able to have a healthy discussion around what should and shouldn't be done with the data, with all voices being considered. One thing that I have discovered when working with organizations with a healthy data culture is that they have a very customer-centric approach. They typically have a deep understanding of customer needs, preferences and behaviours, allowing them to naturally champion the rights of the customer when using their data. Often there will be a customer data champion who will work with the organization to ensure that when data is used, the customer's interests and privacy are protected. This may be a formal role in either marketing or product teams that is responsible for how customer data is used or an informal role adopted by one or more employees who ensure the business uses customer data in an ethical and responsible way.

This also has the benefit of empowering employees to collect customer data, knowing that their organization will not misuse that data. It also helps an organization to really question why it needs to collect that data, rather than just looking at things through a compliance lens. A good data culture allows a more balanced view, weighing up the benefits to the organization and the customer against potential risks. Whenever I've worked with organizations who want to collect more data, an organization without a healthy data culture will typically have a compliance oversight person or team who has the last say. Trying to convince the business to consider collecting additional customer data becomes extremely difficult and rarely will you receive any senior leadership support. This you will see in highly regulated industries like insurance and banking, where the collection and use of data is more often than not dictated by the legal and compliance team.

With organizations in these regulated industries who have a good data culture, there is much more of a partnership between the business and the compliance/regulatory team, and a willingness to explore how data can be collected and used, without a blanket rejection of any idea to collect data beyond that which is absolutely necessary. A good data culture developed even in a very data-restrictive industry can open up dialogue and debate about what data can be collected and what can be done with it. There is usually a healthy exchange of ideas, and regulatory rules dictating what a business can do with data is often seen as something to comply with for the benefit of the customer and the business, and not something that is used to shut down exploration.

When the General Data Protection Regulation (GDPR) came out, companies with a weak or unhealthy data culture would point to GDPR as a reason for not doing something with data. I have sat in so many meetings where the company's compliance or legal teams have claimed that they cannot even collect visitor data from websites because of GDPR. In companies where a good data culture exists, the company's compliance team is more likely to provide guidance on what is or is not possible, allowing the business to decide what it wants to do without exposing itself to unnecessary risk.

A poor data culture can undermine the effectiveness of compliance efforts and expose the organization to various risks. To address these issues, organizations need to prioritize the development of a robust data culture that values and ensures responsible data management practices throughout the entire organization. Part of data management practice is establishing good data governance. Here, there is a need for balance, as a good data culture can heighten an organization's realization of what is possible with the data and make them more adventurous. When this happens, the organization needs to be made more aware of data governance guidance so that in their excitement and enthusiasm to want to do more with data they do not do something that could expose them to unnecessary risk.

Therefore, a balance is needed when a good data culture has evolved in an organization, for data governance practices which proactively allow the business to experiment and explore. In an organization with a poor data culture, what you will typically witness is that data governance is not given much thought in the planning stages and is mostly seen as a documentation process, keeping a record of what data the organization has and what it means.

Data governance should serve as a critical enabler for organizations by providing a structured framework and set of processes to ensure the effective management, quality and security of data assets. An organization with a good data culture would have clear policies, standards and guidelines, and data governance establishes a foundation for consistent and reliable data practices across the organization. This consistency, in turn, enhances decision-making processes by ensuring that all stakeholders have access to accurate and relevant information. Moreover, data governance promotes transparency, accountability and compliance with regulatory requirements, fostering a culture of trust among employees, customers and partners.

Happier customers

A lot of the data collected by an organization is usually derived from customer activity, and a strong data culture plays a pivotal role in building trust with customers by fostering transparency, accountability and responsible data practices. When customers perceive that an organization values and prioritizes data integrity and security, it instils confidence in the handling of their personal information. A good data culture ensures that data is collected, stored and used ethically, with clear communication about how customer information will be used, stored and shared. This transparency not only meets regulatory requirements, as organizations with a good data culture will make their use of data public in their terms and conditions, but also establishes a foundation for trust, as customers feel more informed and in control of their data.

My experience of working in organizations with a good data culture is that they are confident in making public what they will be doing with the customer data. If it was something that they felt was unethical then they would not be doing it and definitely not be making this information public. These organizations are also happy to periodically update customers on how their data is used and even offer them the opportunity to opt out if they are no longer confident in the company storing and using their data or no longer want their data to be used by the company. This is quite an interesting situation, as by being this confident and transparent, they are also in a position where customers are willing to part with more data.

I have yet to see a company that is transparent about what it does with customer data find that the majority of their customers opt out of their data being collected and used. If anything, customers are more likely to share their data as this is an outward expression of an organization with a healthy data culture. When an organization transparently communicates its use of customer data, it cultivates trust and confidence among its customers. By openly sharing information on data collection, processing and security measures, the organization demonstrates a commitment to ethical practices and respect for customers' privacy. This transparency not only shows they are aligning with regulatory standards but also empowers customers by providing them with a clear understanding of how their data contributes to personalized experiences or impacts their interactions with the organization. Customers, feeling informed and in control, are more likely to engage positively with the company, fostering a sense of trust that is foundational for long-term relationships.

Final thoughts

Working towards and maintaining a good data culture as described in this book is hard. However, once an organization has established good practices that foster a healthy data culture, they will find that it brings about transformative changes in the practices of the organization by fostering a mindset where data is seen as a strategic asset. When data is seen as a strategic asset, then investment by the organization in this area becomes less about proving its value, and more about understanding the risks of not doing so. When data-driven decision-making practices embed themselves in the organization's overall culture, it helps the organization to use data to detect issues early, identify opportunities for improvement, explore and experiment with new ideas and drive continuous organizational learning.

Moreover, something that I have seen time and time again is that a strong data culture instils a sense of collaboration and accountability within the organization. Cross-functional teams work more effectively by sharing data and insights, breaking down silos that hinder innovation. This is mainly because data serves as an objective and impartial lens through which to measure performance, success and failure. Senior management, in turn, sets clear expectations for what is required of the data leader, the data team and the data, investing in data infrastructure and tools. It also means that when key individuals who were critical to the establishment of the data culture leave it should have very minimal impact on the data culture of the organization as a whole and others should know what good looks like.

Overall, a good data culture not only improves the efficiency and effectiveness of internal processes but also positions the company to be more agile, responsive to market changes, and equipped to maintain a competitive edge in the dynamic business landscape. Developing a strong and healthy data culture is a must for all organizations. Every business is a data business. They collect a vast amount of data, which if not collected, stored, analysed and used appropriately will lead to them falling behind their competitors or failing to be relevant to their customers. Many organizations are finding that after all the efficiency and gains digital transformation has delivered, they are still on par with their competitors and only data can help them differentiate, compete and win.

INDEX

The index is filed in alphabetical, word-by-word order. Numbers in main headings are filed as spelt out in full; acronyms are filed as presented. Page locators in *italics* denote information contained within a figure or table.

Looking for another book?

Explore our award-winning
books from global business
experts in Business Strategy

Scan the code to browse

www.koganpage.com/business-
strategy

Also from Kogan Page

Data, analytics and research

NAVIGATING SUSTAINABILITY DATA

How organizations can use ESG data to secure their future

Sherry Madera

ISBN: 9781398612242

BE DATA ANALYTICAL

HOW TO USE ANALYTICS TO TURN DATA INTO VALUE

JORDAN MORROW

ISBN: 9781398609280

2nd Edition

DATA ETHICS

Practical strategies for implementing ethical information management and governance

Katherine O'Keefe & Daragh O Brien

ISBN: 9781398610279

BE DATA LITERATE

THE DATA LITERACY SKILLS EVERYONE NEEDS TO SUCCEED

JORDAN MORROW

ISBN: 9781789668018

2ND EDITION

DATA STRATEGY

HOW TO PROFIT FROM A WORLD OF BIG DATA, ANALYTICS AND ARTIFICIAL INTELLIGENCE

BERNARD MARR

ISBN: 9781398602588

THE ENTERPRISE BIG DATA FRAMEWORK

Building Critical Capabilities to Win in the Data Economy

JAN-WILLEM MIDDELBURG

ISBN: 9781398601710

www.koganpage.com

KoganPage

Printed in the USA
CPSIA information can be obtained
at www.ICGtesting.com
LVHW051542040524
779261LV00012B/338

9 781398 614208